METASKILLS

The Spiritual Art of Therapy

METASKILLS
The Spiritual Art of Therapy

By

Amy Mindell, Ph.D.

Introduced
By
Arnold Mindell

1995
NEW FALCON PUBLICATIONS
TEMPE, ARIZONA U.S.A.

International Standard Book Number: 1-56184-119-6
Library of Congress Catalog Card Number: 94-68554

First Edition 1995

Cover art by S. Jason Black

The paper used in this publication meets the minimum require-ments of the American National Standard for Permanence of Paper for Printed Library Materials Z39.48-1984

Address all inquiries to:
New Falcon Publications
1739 East Broadway Road Suite 1-277
Tempe, Arizona 85282 U.S.A.
(or)
1605 East Charleston Blvd.
Las Vegas, NV 89104 U.S.A.

Also by Amy Mindell

Riding the Horse Backwards
Process Oriented Theory and Practice

with Arnold Mindell
(Penguin(Arkana) 1992)

TABLE OF CONTENTS

ACKNOWLEDGMENTS

Two individuals have been extremely important in the development of this work. My husband, Arny Mindell, is my friend, lover and finest teacher. His pioneering research, development and practice of process oriented psychology have inspired this book. I just love him. For me, his work with individuals, couples and groups all around the world brings together spirituality, art, science and therapy in a most precious way. He has supported me in carrying out every part of this work.

A second influential person was one of Carl Jung's greatest students, Barbara Hannah, who died in 1986 at the age of 95. Although we never met, I have felt her spirit repeatedly throughout the writing of this text. From what I know of her, she was an elegant model of a woman who thoroughly trusted and followed her feeling life both in the therapy room and in private. Her example has inspired me to do the same. I feel she would be behind this work through dreams because she knew that feelings that arise in therapy, both in the client and therapist, are core to the development of a meaningful and passionate life.

I would also like to thank my colleagues and friends Dawn Menken, Robert King, Nisha Zenoff, Regula Zust, Marvin Surkin and Martin Vosseler for their insightful reading and critique of my work. Jan Dworkin was particularly helpful to me in sorting out my ideas and giving me new insights, and structural ideas. Pearl and Carl Mindell gave me very helpful feedback. The Swiss process work community was instrumental in providing a container in which these ideas could grow. Thanks to Dr. Ogawa, Yoshiko Tanaoka, Tim McLean, Yukio Fujimi, Kazuko Sato and our Japanese students for inviting us to work in Japan and teaching us so much about Japanese culture. Keido Fukushima, the Zen master of the Tofukuji Monastery in Kyoto, through his own delightful and radiant metaskills of humor, detachment and compassion, clarified some of the central concepts of Zen. Thanks also to Slava Tsapkin and Fyodor Vashiliuk for their insights into metaskills and Russian psychotherapy. Leslie Heizer was a wonderful and skilled editor. Thanks to Ingrid Schuitevoerder for her typing in the last moments when this work suddenly disappeared from my computer. Thanks also to Nasira Alma for her important editing help. Sonja Straub was instrumental in helping to carve out teaching methods for aspects of this work. And special thanks goes to students and colleagues in the process work community around the world who have helped clarify, test and explore the ideas in this book.

Acknowledgement is also given to the following for their kind permission to quote from the cited works: Celestial Arts, Box 7327, Berkeley, CA 94707 for *Embrace Tiger, Return to Mountain: The Essence of Tai Chi* © 1973, 1987 by Chunglian Al Huang; Thames and Hudson, London, England for *Tao: The Chinese Philosophy of Time and Change* © 1973 by R. Rawson & L. Legezo and *Martial Arts: The Spiritual Dimension* © 1981 by P. Payne; New Directions Publications for *The Way of Chuang Tzu* by T. Merton © 1965 by The Abbey of Gethsemaine, ME; Alfred A. Knopf, Inc. for *Tao Te Ching* by Lao Tsu, © 1972 translated by, and copyright by Jane English and Gia-Fu Feng; Oxford University Press for *What is Psychotherapy?* by Sidney Bloch © 1982; Penguin Books, Ltd., London, England for *Working With the Dreaming Body* © 1986 and *River's Way: The Process Science of the Dreambody* © 1985 by Arnold Mindell.

FOREWORD

by Arnold Mindell

I would love to give an objective introduction to this book, but I know I cannot. Amy Mindell, my most beloved teacher, is a walking bundle of what she calls metaskills. Something about her is healing, though until she wrote this book, I did not quite know what it was. She is full of the compassion and playfulness she describes in Chapters Five and Seven.

Metaskill is a new concept in therapy. It pulls together everything we know about the subtle feeling abilities of healers. As Amy points out, metaskills are the bottom line to psychotherapy. Jung said somewhere that the therapist is her or his own best formula. If he lived today, he would have to say that therapists' metaskills determine how we affect someone else's personal development, independently of what theories, models and skills we have been taught.

This is why some people are Jungian even though they may have studied Gestalt, and some apparently Jungian people are Gestaltists, depending upon their metaskills. Some Freudians and Jungians, body movement people and Gestalt therapists are process oriented, depending upon their relationship to Taoism.

Amy's ideas cut across age groups and education, national and personal characteristics. They are an important contribution to the future of therapy. Clients and therapists of every school will have to consider metaskills basic to self-knowledge. Our knowledge of these metaskills, as Amy points out, predicts how and if we can help others.

By encouraging me to study these feeling skills, Amy has helped me more than any other teacher, to understand myself.

Arny Mindell
Yachats, Oregon, 1994

Section I

METASKILLS

Chapter One

MOON IN THE WATER

Deep spiritual attitudes and beliefs manifest in therapy and in everyday life. This book explores the ways that therapists express, through their feeling attitudes, their fundamental beliefs about life. These attitudes permeate and shape all of the therapist's apparent techniques. Conceptually, I raise these essential, underlying feelings of the therapist to "skills" that must and can be studied and cultivated. I call these new skills "metaskills." In essence, this book focuses on the spiritual art of therapy.

As you study and focus upon the subtle feeling level of your work, you become involved in an artistic and spiritual discipline. You transform your deepest beliefs into living reality as life and therapy become creative, mysterious and awesome experiences. The study of metaskills brings together the earth and sky of therapy and of everyday life.

✶✶✶✶✶

When this manuscript was almost completed, my husband Arny and I took our third trip to Japan, where we had been invited to give training workshops in process oriented psychology (process work). We were delighted to find that many of the central tenets of process work were deeply rooted in Japanese thought.

We spent much of our time exploring Japanese culture and found ourselves walking one day in the ancient city of Nara, the first capital of Japan. It was a lovely November day.

As Arny and I strolled through Nara Park, we came upon an age-old shrine amidst the deer and yak. Walking up the stairs full of stone lanterns and bright red sweeping roofs, we stumbled upon a fortune-telling booth. The sign read: *Fortunes in English.* "Why not?" we thought.

Arny was already at the booth, shaking the wooden container until a thin wooden stick emerged from the tiny hole on the end. It read: "Number 9, Great Good Fortune."

My luck was not as favorable on that particular afternoon. I pulled: "Number 11, Limited Good Fortune." I was not surprised. I had been struggling for days with the completion of this manuscript, which I had originally entitled "Moon in the Water."

The next lines jumped out as if they had been waiting for me:

No matter how hard one tries,
it is impossible to grasp the moon's reflection
seen on the surface of a pond.

My god! I had come to Japan and rediscovered the first title of this book! I had chosen this title after reading many books on Zen Buddhist philosophy and having found this Zen phrase[1] beautifully descriptive of my thesis: that therapists have the potential to manifest their deepest spiritual beliefs (the moon) in living practice (the water). And that all of us are like the moon's reflection in the water in that shining moment when we manifest our deepest beliefs in the living and flowing reality of everyday life.

[1]Shunryu Suzuki, *Zen Mind, Beginner's Mind: Informal Talks on Zen Meditation and Practice*, New York: Weatherhill, 1970, p.127.

But what did this fortune mean? Should I stop trying to complete this book and, as the fortune stated, "await the proper time, and it will surely come"? The fortune further suggested that I should not lose hope and should not force my way ahead.

That evening I pondered the significance of such a synchronicity. As I began to pack my suitcase, I remembered the Zen Roshi we had met earlier in the day. What a delightful man! He was the embodiment of all that I had imagined of a Zen master—enormously happy, laughing, kind, and terribly direct! His actions were a living reflection of Zen teachings.

Then I discovered the fan that this Roshi had presented to us as a gift. During our visit, he suddenly disappeared out one of the sliding doors of the temple meeting room. A few minutes later he reappeared with this fan. While he was out of the room, he had inscribed the fan with his own calligraphy. I had not had a chance to look at the fan earlier. Now, sitting in our hotel room, I was once again startled as I read the translation of his Japanese characters:

Dip water, hold the moon in your hands.

Well, I was running into the moon and the water everywhere! In true Zen fashion I found myself involved in a paradoxical koan. Is it or is it not possible to grasp the moon in the water? Can I, or can I not complete this work? Is it possible or is it not possible to write about an aspect of psychotherapy that is so illusive, yet so crucial to a therapist's work? How can I describe the subtle feeling background to therapy that normally is only implied in a therapist's actions? How can I possibly write about the way that our spiritual beliefs manifest in the actions of our ordinary lives?

I swirled in my own paradoxical confusion. Perhaps it is true: there is no time to catch these feelings, just as there is no pause between the moon's appearance and its reflection in the water.

I deliberated. Is this not a contradiction? How could I describe special feeling attitudes of the therapist if, as I imagined, they cannot be taught but must arise spontaneously? How could these feeling attitudes be turned into a skill? I wanted to talk about metaskills that are hinted at by the ancient Taoists but realized that most of us, most of the time are not Taoistic at all!

I felt like the bumbling Carlos Castaneda as he describes his apprenticeship with the Yaqui Indian teacher, Don Juan—confused by my intellect, probing territories where the answers always seemed to just slip from under my fingertips. Don Juan tells Carlos:

> 'I talk to you because you make me laugh,' he said. 'You remind me of some bushy-tailed rats of the desert that get caught when they stick their tails in holes trying to scare other rats away in order to steal their food. You get caught in your own questions. Watch out! Sometimes those rats yank their tails off trying to pull themselves free.'[1]

My tail was getting caught over and over again! I was losing perspective, fearing that I would lose all my senses, yet felt compelled to discover the answers and complexity behind these riddles.

Luckily, something began to change. A few days later I had a dream about my husband Arny and a very old lumberman from the Oregon Coast. The two of them got out of a pickup truck, walked over to a frozen lake, took out their pickaxes and started to chop away at the ice. The water began to flow once again! My tendency to see things as this or that was beginning to loosen and thaw!

I then realized how important it was to write about the "feeling" background to psychotherapy. This subtle back-

---

[1]Carlos Castaneda, *A Separate Reality,* London: Penguin, 1973, p. 89.

ground, whether conscious or not, carries great significance. It is in this atmosphere that we discover the therapist's feelings about life, nature and human development. It is through these feelings and the atmosphere they create that the therapist's spiritual values spring to life. Often these most significant beliefs and feelings are not clearly defined, yet strongly influence a therapist's interactions. They loom like a hidden mist which colors and pervades the therapist's techniques. The client feels these attitudes whether the therapist uses them consciously or not. And yet, is this not what psychotherapy is about? Isn't there something behind psychotherapy which is spiritual, which addresses the basis of life and our reasons for living?

I chose the term "metaskills" to signify the ongoing awareness and use of our attitudes in a more *conscious* way in practice. Metaskills are like the moon's reflection in the water. They are the vehicles that animate our normal techniques and allow our deepest beliefs to take root. As skills and metaskills merge, the fabric of a therapist's work is woven with her deepest beliefs.

In my therapeutic training I realized that process oriented psychology was, for me, not a combination of its skills and techniques, but something more fundamental. Its techniques could never really describe its essence. While some therapeutic approaches stress behavioral change or insight, I was attracted to process work's belief in the Tao—that numinous, unexpected mystery which fills us as individuals and groups with the sense of awe.[1] I was excited by process work's determination to embrace the disavowed aspects of our experiences, and its efforts to go beyond solutions to our problems towards more sustainable approaches to body symptoms, near-death experiences, relationship issues,

---

[1]See Amy Mindell & Arny Mindell's *Riding the Horse Backwards: Process Oriented Theory and Practice*, London: Penguin(Arkana), 1982, Chapter 1.

extreme states, and large group conflict situations. I felt that its emphasis on the political and social context of therapeutic work was crucial to the evolution of therapy and the building of a sustainable world.

I was fascinated by the way that the process oriented therapist's feeling attitudes such as fluidity, compassion, humor, playfulness, and shamanism allowed these basic beliefs to come to life in practice. I elevate these feeling attitudes to the level of a skill appreciating and cultivating them with as much love and depth as ordinary techniques. The concept of metaskills implies a new art form or discipline that can be fostered and studied.

I realized that these "feeling-oriented" attitudes of the therapist can never be accurately described in words. It is true that, just as there is no interval between the appearance of the moon and its reflection in the water, there is also no time to capture the essence of the therapist's attitudes. The paradoxical Zen phrases remind me that my task is to hint at the existence and significance of metaskills, giving them names and descriptions which are only momentarily useful, knowing that all of this may change with time and the development of therapy.

Metaskills flow into one another and do not have clearly definable boundaries. They can be described only through analogies. Therefore the reader will find some overlap and repetition. And yet, I must dip my hands in the water and hold the moon for a fleeting moment to share its reflection with you.

The practical cases which follow are derived from therapy sessions but nevertheless illustrate how all of us can bring our feeling attitudes into our conscious lives. The examples and explanations show how to transform compassionate feelings into interactions with ourselves and with others, how to bring playfulness, detachment and humor into our everyday activities, how to become lazy and precise, shamanic and scientific, and how to open up to aspects of ourselves and our world which we tend to ignore or throw away. In this way, we all become the "moon in the water." Life becomes a continually evolving, creative, unpredictable, and numinous experience.

The Sections

In Section One I define the concept of metaskills and show how this study provides a new method of understanding and organizing the vast field of psychotherapy as we know it today. I discuss the way in which our attitudes and feelings bring our deepest beliefs to life, and show how the concept of metaskills is beautifully expressed in Eastern spiritual traditions.

Section Two takes a closer look at process oriented metaskills in practice. For this section, I have chosen to focus primarily on case examples from the work of my husband, Arny Mindell, the founder of process oriented psychology. Though I, too, manifest many of the feeling attitudes discussed in this book when I interact with clients, it is easier for me to be objective about someone else's work. The examples in this section poignantly exemplify the metaskills that I highlight in each chapter. Each metaskill is amplified through analogies to either Eastern traditions, teachings of Don Juan, and/or modern physics.

The case examples in this work focus mainly on individual therapy and are from process work seminars. In these cases I refer to the therapist as "Arny" and "he." Elsewhere, for balance and simplicity, I often refer to the prototypical therapist as "she."

The reader should know that, in essence, the metaskills described in these chapters are inherent in any person who has a Taoist orientation to life; that is, anyone interested in following the ebb and flow of nature. These metaskills are found in many therapeutic systems and in the work of individual therapists who share the belief in the wisdom of nature. As far as I know, the metaskills which I examine in Section II appear in individuals all over the world, independent of cultural or ethnic backgrounds, though each person manifests these metaskills in his or her own personal way. The examples show a few of the ways in which these Taoistic feelings express themselves in practice.

In Section Three I approach the question of learning metaskills. Is it possible, and how do we do it? In essence, the therapist, like the client, is on a path of spiritual development. What does this spiritual discipline entail? I suggest that the concept of metaskills may lead us to a new definition of a therapist—someone not confined to a traditional role but free to follow her changing feelings. She becomes an artist, scientist, shaman, meditator, spiritual teacher or fool as she rides her feelings, uses her skills and simultaneously watches and adjusts to the feedback of her client. This therapist is as fluid and free as she hopes the client will be. She models the ability to ebb and flow with nature. Finally, I discuss how the study of metaskills inspires all of us to bring our basic hopes and dreams into everyday life.

Chapter Two

THE EARTH
OF PSYCHOTHERAPY

Therapy is not simply a matter of technique or theory or philosophy. It is a matter of the therapist's feelings for herself and others. What the therapist feels and how she uses these feelings in her work defines who she is and how she responds to life. Her deepest beliefs and feelings are the earth from which all techniques spring.

The therapist's world view and attitudes make a direct statement about human interactions. Her feeling interactions in turn create lasting effects on the people she works with and their subsequent relationships. We must ask ourselves: "What kind of world do we want?" and "How do we manifest this world view in practice?"

Without conscious awareness of her changing feeling attitudes, the therapist may act depressed or superior. She may get attached to one particular feeling mode and subsequently complain of "burn out." A therapist may act wise, for example, when she feels like a fool. She might sit back in a detached way when something inside of her would like to be more active. How can she hope that her client will become free if she herself is not?

This book stresses this feeling background to therapeutic work which implicitly or explicitly influences the quality, tone and atmosphere of human interactions. It refers to past efforts that have attempted to identify the ground or central feelings that are crucial in therapeutic work. Yet this work also propels us into the future in three important ways.

First, it emphasizes the conscious use of feeling attitudes in practice. Feelings are elevated to metaskills that can be studied, researched and deeply cared for. By metaskills, I do not mean that we should focus on the *ideal* feeling attitudes of the therapist but instead concentrate and study the *actual* feelings that a therapist has from moment to moment. The task is to make these attitudes conscious and useful in the therapeutic situation.

Secondly, it shows that a therapist's ability to move fluidly between various feeling attitudes as they arise gives her access to the very basis of various schools of psychotherapy. Strict classification among forms of therapy begins to break down as we study how feeling attitudes connect or distance therapists from one another regardless of their school of origin. The study of metaskills suggests a new organization of the field of psychotherapy.

Thirdly, this work shows that the therapist's basic feeling attitudes mirror her deepest attitudes toward life, nature and human development. As she makes these feelings conscious she manifests her spiritual beliefs in living practice. *Hence, therapy becomes a spiritual task.*

✳✳✳✳✳

Before describing the concept of metaskills in greater depth, let me backtrack for a moment and describe the evolution of this work and the role of metaskills in modern psychotherapy.

In 1989, my husband Arny and I were living and working as resident scholars at Esalen Institute in Big Sur, California. Our access to the Esalen video library afforded a welcome overview of the work of many prominent therapists. We watched "in action" many therapists about whom I had only read previously. It was thrilling to see their styles, their particular nuances and the way their unique personalities mingled with their therapeutic skills. I was excited to see how theoretical ideas and techniques came to life in living practice.

I remember watching a video tape of Fritz Perls, the founder of Gestalt therapy, and then a tape of Dick Price, a Gestalt therapist and former co-owner of Esalen. Both men identified themselves as Gestalt therapists and used similar Gestalt tools. Yet, the way they practiced Gestalt therapy during these particular sessions was radically different. Perls had a confrontational and directive style while Price, who had an interest in Vipassana meditation, was more passive, open and gentle in his interactions with his clients.

This made a strong impression on me and raised a fundamental question: If the *way* these men worked with people was so different, were they both practicing Gestalt therapy? If their theory and techniques were similar but their attitudes so different, were they actually from the same school? Is it simply a matter of difference in personal style or can we discover through their actions something fundamentally different about their approaches to life and therapy? I wanted to focus precisely on the way we practice therapy and what living practice reveals about our deepest beliefs.

Imagine for a moment two people who use a hammer. One of these people uses a lot of force when pounding on a nail. The other uses a more gentle and cautious approach. The tool is the same, but the way of using the tool is very different and mirrors something about the individual's beliefs about hammering and the task at hand. Even though both people perform the same task—pounding a nail in the wall—the whole flavor and ambiance of this hammering is different. This insight is a first step in distinguishing techniques from the attitudes behind them.

Techniques can never really fully describe what we do. They are empty vessels which can be applied neutrally. Students in the middle of their studies sometimes look quite mechanical because they attempt to apply techniques in a neutral fashion. It is as though they have picked the flower out of the earth and used it without reference to its roots and origin.

Individual Therapists

The study of metaskills suggests viewing the work of individual psychotherapists in a new way. I may, for example, prefer one practitioner of a given school while not being drawn to another. This is not necessarily because their techniques are different but because the attitudes which pervade those techniques match or do not match something fundamental that I feel about nature and life as a whole. Some people attribute this to the therapist's style, but I think there is more to it. There is too little focus on the actual, momentary attitudes of the therapist and what they say about the practice of therapy and the field of psychotherapy as a whole.

Let's consider a different situation. Many people who see process oriented psychology (process work) for the first time say, "Oh, I am doing the same thing." Yet they have been trained in a very different school of psychotherapy thousands of miles away. After talking with such people, I realized that what they were referring to, without necessarily having an in-depth understanding of process work, was the attitude that a given process oriented therapist had towards the client rather than specific techniques and skills. Therefore, anyone with similar beliefs and feelings about people might feel that he or she is "doing the same thing" or is directly related in a feeling way to what is happening, even if his or her skills are quite different.

A particular body worker or a massage therapist whose central attitude is one of openness toward nature and the unique process of any client, may feel closely allied with a process worker, even though her techniques are quite different. Another body worker from the same school and who uses the same techniques may have a totally different feeling approach. She may feel that the client's body needs changing and reforming because of old, negative patterns. Her attitudes toward her client reflect this belief. She may not feel allied with the process worker or even her own colleague. Both methods are important, yet we must question the assumption that these two body work practitioners have the same fundamental beliefs or belong to the same school of thought.

The Ground of Psychotherapy

By looking at these basic beliefs and feelings of the therapist we are confronting the very ground of psychotherapy—the mother, the earth, from which it springs; the container which holds and produces all other skills.

There are, of course many different kinds of earth. One type of earth is very hard and solid, another craggy, another soggy or marshy. Some earth is gentle while other is dry. Some earth exists above the tree line, soaring high in a detached way. Some is mystically bound to a dark and mysterious rainforest. Of course, it is not possible to exactly differentiate one type of earth from another. Each piece flows into the next, as each attitude of the therapist flows into other attitudes, and many schools of therapy overlap with one another.

From this earth, from our basic beliefs and attitudes, spring forth various plants (techniques). It is possible to remove a plant (technique) from its soil and transplant it in another spot. In so doing, however, the original ground or feeling may be lost.

For example, a process oriented belief that "nature is wise if we are able to consciously unfold its contents" gives birth to a technique called "amplification" (on which there is more in Chapter Six). Amplification is a method for strengthening our experiences so they can develop and unfold. Someone could come by and pull up this "amplification" plant and use it without reference to its original feeling but this would be an altogether different approach. It is the original earth that finally radiates through our techniques and affects the people we interact with.

Redefining the Field of Psychotherapy

While there are different and separate schools of therapy, practitioners of certain therapies are connected to practitioners from other schools more by the earth or the attitudes they embody, the *way* they work, than by their particular schools of thought. On the other hand, if two practitioners from the same school have very different attitudes, but similar techniques, perhaps they actually belong to very different schools.

This notion is found in Sidney Bloch's *What Is Psychotherapy*. Bloch says that each therapist develops his or her particular manner of working, which "may be challenging or supportive, authoritative or permissive, active or passive, opaque or self disclosing, detached or involved..."[1] He says that the style a therapist develops may have very little relationship to the professional school from which that therapist has come.

> The eventual pattern that typifies a therapist's style may bear little or no relationship to his professional school. Two Jungian therapists for example may claim to use a similar theoretical approach but exhibit radically different styles. Moreover, one of them may be closer in

---

[1] S. Bloch, *What is Psychotherapy,* Oxford & New York: Oxford University Press, 1982, p. 52.

style to a therapist belonging to another school than to his own colleague.[1]

I believe the current overlapping of psychotherapies and the tendency toward eclecticism have much to do with the need to define and categorize schools by the feelings the therapist has about life and the way these are conveyed in practice. Indeed, someone practicing Jungian psychology may, feeling-wise, be more of a Freudian than a Jungian. A Gestalt therapist may be more of a Behaviorist than a Gestaltist depending upon her or his basic attitudes towards people. Some process oriented therapists may be fundamentally more behaviorist than process oriented if we really observe *how* they do their work.

Perhaps our categorization of psychotherapies needs a fundamental change. By focusing on the *way* of therapy, we may see more connections among some therapists and more divergence among others than we have so far realized. As we focus more deeply on the feeling quality of therapeutic work and what therapists actually do in practice, we discover more about their actual beliefs. Such a study may point to the need for a new understanding and organization of the field psychotherapy.

What We Actually Do

The focus on attitudes suggests further study of what we *actually* do in therapy. It is one thing to espouse certain beliefs and quite another to manifest these in practice or in everyday life. As Bloch says,

> Customarily, therapists are much more aware of their theoretical position than of their actual behavior with patients... [Therapists] need to pay more attention to the way in which they actually work with their patients.[2]

---

[1]Ibid.
[2]Bloch, op. cit., p. 53.

My research suggests that it is not enough to emulate the important qualities of a therapist or other important people in our lives or behave "as if" we have these qualities. For better or worse, it is not possible to program ourselves to have specific feelings like empathy or genuineness. This work stresses the importance of the *awareness* of the feeling attitudes that arise spontaneously inside of us as opposed to *prescribing* which feelings to have.

Jeffrey Masson addresses this issue in his work *Against Therapy.*[1] In a discussion of Carl Rogers' work, Masson asks why we assume that the therapist actually feels the particular attitudes that Rogers believes are important in a healing environment. The desire for a therapist to have unconditional regard for his or her clients, he says, does not mean that the therapist will feel this regard at all times.

Masson raises a central question. Future studies may focus on the exact attitudes which can be seen in videotaped or live sessions of various therapists working with their clients. If we desire particular feeling qualities in therapists, does that mean that they can simply act that way? If the therapist does not feel the desired emotions, what then does he or she actually feel? How can he or she use these feelings fruitfully in the therapeutic context? What can we learn?

The Importance of Attitudes

To grasp the significance of our feeling attitudes, think for a moment about teachers, friends and mentors who have been influential in your life. What was it about them that was important to you? What remains with you even if you do not have contact with them anymore? What was impressive—what about that particular person had impact on you? Was it not a special feeling quality, the way they

---

[1] J. Masson, *Against Therapy: Emotional Tyranny and the Myth of Psychological Healing,* New York: Atheneum, 1988.

treated you and others? Was it not their outlook on life which permeated their work and interactions with people?

I imagine that the aspect of these people that stayed with you most strongly was not necessarily their skills but the *way* they went about life. Did not their attitudes mirror deep beliefs inside of yourself?

Think for a moment about painters, musicians or dancers who have inspired you. Is there something about them that goes way beyond the bounds of their techniques? Is there a feeling quality which reminds you of something which you treasure deep inside yourself?

I remember sitting with a Native American elder about a year ago. She did not speak much. She sat quietly and radiated the kind of depth and compassion and relationship to nature that I longed for. Her attitude towards life struck a deep chord inside of me and has stayed with me ever since. It was not *what* she did but *how* she acted that was meaningful to me. Her presence and her attitude towards life were a great source of inspiration for me.

Students of psychotherapy may be attracted to a particular school or individual practitioner because that school's or individual's beliefs mirror something inside themselves. When I first began to speak to my students and colleagues about the importance of attitudes in therapy, many students said, "Yes, that is why I am involved in process work. The techniques are important but it is the essence and feeling behind the work that I am really attracted to."

Implicit Attitudes and Feelings

Metaskills are a central ingredient in therapeutic work. However, more often than not, feelings and attitudes and the background ideology from which they spring, are only implied in our work.

Explicit or not, the attitudes we have toward people cannot be disguised or hidden; they create a strong atmosphere. Our attitudes permeate the way we talk, greet our clients, move, sit in our chairs, and the way we use our techniques.

In fact, even if we have good ideas or skills, using them with the wrong feeling will produce the wrong psychology or adverse effects. A doctor can heal or make you sick depending upon personal attitudes and the feelings that she or he has towards you. Some people simply make you feel well when you are in their presence, while others make you want to run away.

Since our attitudes slip out through our actions, the client will know if we respect him/her, if we think he/she should change, if we are, in essence, interested in existential questions or temporal reality. A client may feel misunderstood if a therapist is unaware of the social structures and attitudes that influence his or her life. In other words, the "way" in which a therapist works reveals, either implicitly or explicitly, her underlying beliefs about life, about social and political issues, about personal development and its relationship to the world, and the nature of therapy.

An attitude of intensity may, for example, reflect a background sentiment about the serious nature of life. The tendency to push as a therapist may reflect the belief that people grow more if they are pushed from the outside. An attitude of anxiety which makes the client feel you want to cure him/her may mirror a belief that people are innately sick and in need of healing. The tendency to sit back and take it easy may indicate that the therapist believes in getting out of the way to allow nature to take its course. On the other hand, if this is done with indifference it might reflect a lack of interest. Humor in a given moment may express a detached attitude toward all events in life. The tendency of a therapist to want to control events may reveal a belief that nature is chaotic and needs to be tamed.

A therapist's constant empathy and warmth may indicate a belief that people grow more easily if they have someone who truly understands them. Remaining neutral and outside of direct relationship with the client may point towards a belief that people need non-interference and neutrality in which to project their inner lives. The attitude that views all experiences as inner phenomena may reveal a world view in which individual reflection is the sole or crucial route towards development. An attitude which connects inner life with social phenomena could reveal a view of the inseparability of individual life, culture, society and history.

Any of these attitudes may be useful in a given moment or situation. Any therapist may go through a number of these feeling qualities in any given session. Normally these feelings remain unconscious influences which pervade our interactions. Therefore, a therapist may convey any of these feelings without realizing it, noticing its effect, or making it useful to her client. Consciously using our attitudes means that we represent them with awareness and, consequently, have the freedom to follow them or let them go depending on the momentary therapist-client interaction. Without this awareness, our attitudes simply imply world views and beliefs that are not fully represented or made useful in our work. We may remain fixed in one feeling attitude without access to any of the other array of feelings inside of ourselves.

Attitudes in Therapy

The importance of feeling attitudes in psychotherapy has been recognized and documented by many researchers and therapists. In his book *Persuasion and Healing*, Jerome D. Frank says:

> Although the therapist's training and his class position relative to that of his patient affect the therapeutic

relationship, personal characteristics and attitudes of therapist and patient may well be more important.[1]

Many desirable attitudes and qualities of the therapist have been suggested by researchers of psychotherapy and counseling ranging from warmth to empathy, to personal power, a willingness to make mistakes, to honesty.[2] Most would agree that a sense of empathy and understanding are central to psychotherapy.

Many schools of psychotherapy espouse specific feeling attitudes that they deem particularly important. Schools such as traditional psychoanalysis value the therapist's neutrality.[3] A neo-Freudian, Karen Horney stressed the analyst's attention, her inner freedom, her ingenuity, and her "fingertip feelings."[4] Behavior therapy stresses learning theory and a therapeutic relationship in which the therapist is "more directive and more concerned ... and serves as a source of personal support."[5]

---

[1] Jerome D. Frank, *Persuasion and Healing*, Baltimore: The Johns Hopkins University Press, 1973, p. 183.

[2] See R. Carkhuff & B. Berenson, *Beyond Counseling and Therapy*, New York: Holt, Rinehart & Winston, 1977, p. 9.

R. Cartwright & B. Lerner, "Empathy, Need to Change and Improvement with Psychotherapy," *Journal of Consulting Psychology*, 1963. Vol. 27, No. 2, pp. 138-144.

G. Corey, M. Corey & P. Callahan, 3rd ed., *Issues and Ethics in the Helping Professions*, Pacific Grove, CA: Brooks/Cover, 1988, p. 48.

J. Frank, "The Dynamics of the Psychotherapeutic Relationship: Determinants and Effects of the Therapist's Influence." In *Psychiatry*, 1959. Vol. 36, Sept. 1979, pp. 1125-1136.

[3] H. Blum, "Psychoanalysis" in *Psychotherapist's Casebook: Theory and Technique in the Practice of Modern Therapies*, eds. Kutash & Wolf, San Francisco: Jossey-Bass, 1986, p. 4.

[4] D. Ingram, "Horney's Psychoanalytic Technique," in Kutash & Wolf, eds., pp. 144-146.

[5] G. Wilson, "Behaviour Therapy" in *Current Psychotherapies*, 3rd ed., ed. Corsini , Illinois: R. E. Peacock Publishers, 1984, p. 254.

Alfred Adler, in his departure from Freud's reductionism, assumed a teleology or purposeful model of human development[1] and spoke of the client-therapist relationship as a "cooperative educational enterprise"[2] in which the therapist is "authentic, must express 'unprejudiced approval' and is empathetic." Empathy, of course, is highly valued in many therapeutic schools. Carl Jung also diverged from traditional psychoanalysis. Based on teleology, Jung viewed the analyst as a "co-partner in discovery" who provides a space for the client to find out about him- or herself. He also stressed the analyst's flexibility in following each client's unique process.[3]

The growth of the humanistic psychology movement in the 1960s, extending Adler and Jung's work, recognized each individual's tendency toward "self-actualization" or the movement of each individual towards positive growth and individuation.[4] These beliefs are mirrored in the attitudes considered desirable in humanistic psychotherapists. Carl Rogers, one of the leading thinkers of this new force in psychology, was perhaps the greatest proponent of the feeling quality of therapy. He identified the attitudes of empathy, caring and genuineness, congruence, unconditional regard, as well as a non-directive approach that allowed the client rather than the therapist to be the leader on the path of development.[5] Rogers went so far as to say

---

[1] Heinz & Rowena Ansbacher, *The Individual Psychology of Alfred Adler,* New York: Basic Books, 1956, p. 94.

[2] Op. cit., 91.

[3] Carl Jung, "Principles of Practical Psychotherapy" in the *Collected Works,* Vol. 16, London: Routledge & Kegan Paul, 1954, p. 10.

[4] R. Walsh & F. Vaughan, *Beyond Ego: Transpersonal Dimensions in Psychology,* Los Angeles: Tarcher, 1980, p. 19.

[5] B. Meador, & C. Rogers, " Person Centered Therapy" in Corsini, op. cit., pp. 144-145.

that embodying these qualities was itself sufficient to produce positive change and growth in the individual.[1]

Expanding outside the parameters of the humanistic movement, transpersonal psychology recognized states of consciousness which extend beyond what had been known as self-actualizing tendencies.[2] Abraham Maslow first spoke of a "transpersonal" realm that was "centered in the cosmos rather than in human needs and interest," and explored higher levels of consciousness.[3] At present there is no one unified system of techniques which all practitioners of transpersonal psychology employ. Transpersonal therapists draw techniques from various Eastern and Western disciplines.

Vaughan and Walsh note that transpersonal therapists are bonded together by a common belief system that creates the "transpersonal context" in which their work is embedded.[4] They are referring, I believe, to the atmosphere which the therapist creates through his or her attitudes and modeling. Vaughan[5] says that "[w]hen ... a therapist identifies with an expanded sense of the self as the source of experience, the potential for healing in the therapeutic relationship is enhanced." James Bugenthal, another transpersonal therapist, asserts, "[t]he most mature psychotherapists are more artists than technicians and they bring to bear a wide variety of sensitivities and skills so their clients can release their latent potentials for fuller living."[6]

---

[1]Sidney Bloch, *What is Psychotherapy?*, Oxford & New York: Oxford University Press, 1982, p. 48.

[2]Walsh & Vaughan, ibid.

[3]Walsh & Vaughan, op. cit., pp. 19-20.

[4]Op. cit., p. 163.

[5]F. Vaughan in Walsh & Vaughan, op. cit., p. 183.

[6]J. Bugental, *The Art of the Psychotherapist*, New York: W. W. Norton, 1987, p. 264.

The Spiritual Art of Therapy

The therapist has a wide variety of feelings and attitudes that rise and fall inside her as she works. She may feel relaxed, anxious, detached, gentle, quiet, fluid, or easy-going. Whether we apply these attitudes consciously or not, they permeate our work and interactions. Why not bring these feelings into our work consciously and usefully? In so doing, we develop as therapists who value and embrace our feelings as they arise in practice.

The concept of metaskills is connected to perennial philosophy—process oriented or Taoistic attitudes—which values the on-going flow of nature. Taoist philosophy says that all events are connected and appear meaningful if they are allowed to unfold. Therefore, the psychotherapist who takes her job as, among other things, a spiritual task, will value and follow the flow of feeling attitudes that surface as she works. These feelings will be welcome as an aspect of nature which asks for recognition and awareness. As she allows them to surface consciously she makes it possible for her deepest beliefs to find footing in everyday practice.

Why the term "metaskills"? The term "meta" implies an outside point of view from which we are able to notice what we are experiencing, which feelings are occurring in any given moment. The term "metaskills," then, refers not only to the feelings that occur while we are working, but to becoming *aware* of these feelings as they arise inside of us. Further, the term "metaskills" implies that, in addition to noticing these attitudes, we pick them up and cull their energy, using our feelings and attitudes in the service of the client.

In other words, "metaskills" does not simply refer to the feelings or attitudes we have as therapists, but places the focus on the conscious use of these attitudes in practice. It demands that the therapist scrutinize her feeling-awareness to notice and ride the various attitudes which come up in her as she works. She may then bring her attitudes *usefully* into her therapeutic interactions and notice the changes and feedback which occur. Finally, she adjusts herself to this feedback and notices how her attitudes change once again. The concept of metaskills demands that the therapist strengthen her feeling awareness and simultaneously use all of her other practical tools in the service of the client.

Metaskills and Painting

Imagine a painter as she approaches her canvas. She holds the brush, dips it into the colors and is about to paint. She has learned many skills in her training, but now, as she is about to embark on her creative task, what does she feel? Is she gripping the brush tightly with intensity? Transforming her feeling into a metaskill in this moment would mean noticing that she is feeling intense and then using this intensity as the *way* of painting. Her intense attitude begins to pervade her techniques. As her mood changes, she picks up new attitudes and consciously uses these as her guides. Metaskills determine the quality of her work.

If this artist is, on the other hand, gently dabbing her brush in the paint, she will pick up this tendency and produce lines and forms generated by this delicate feeling. If she is feeling erratic, she might paint quickly and furiously with short, punctuated and non-linear motions. These feeling-oriented states intermingle with the various formal techniques she has learned to create her particular style.

Of course, during the creation of any one painting, she may find herself full of a vast array of different feelings. If she becomes aware of these changing feelings and allows them to express themselves on her canvas, she will finish with a collage of differing intensities, colors, styles and forms. These subtle variations in the way she expresses herself through her tools are her "metaskills."

Similarly, the therapist will notice that different feelings and attitudes arise in herself as she is working. If she is consciously able to pick up these tendencies and allow them to speak through her work, she becomes a fluid practitioner who brings her attitudes in usefully. She then notices the feedback from her client and adjusts herself to it. She follows the client and herself, using her feelings, attitudes, and techniques in her work.

An Example

Perhaps a short process work example would be useful. I remember being very touched by a woman who wanted to focus on her breast cancer in one of our Lava Rock Dream Body Clinics on the Oregon coast.[1]

> The woman said that she had a lot of pain but did not talk about it much. She began to work together with Arny as the rest of the seminar participants looked on. At one stage in her work, she began to move and then stopped. She said she was afraid because her movements reminded her of death. Her motions shifted and changed and she said that she was unfamiliar with this kind of experience. Arny, following his feelings, noticed that he was touched, and paused for a moment. He said that he understood how scary this experience must be. They stood quietly together.
>
> Then, noticing his feelings changing, Arny realized that he was curious about her experience. He knew that nature presents itself in often unpredictable ways and wanted to help her unfold this mysterious process. He was also aware that she had stopped at the *edge*, the boundary of her known world. (See Chapter Five).
>
> He asked the woman if she would like to explore her experience just a little more. She hesitated. Noticing the

---

[1]The Lava Rock Clinic occurs twice a year and focuses on chronic and acute body symptoms. The clinic provides a community atmosphere where those with body symptoms are as much the teachers and therapists as they are the clients. The clinic is run by Dr. Max Schuepbach, Arny Mindell and a process work staff.

feedback, Arny paused as well. After a few moments, the woman said she actually would like to find out more about her movement.

She moved her arms, began to arch backwards and started to make noises which increased in volume. Arny accompanied and helped her with this arching movement. In a transformational moment, she screamed out, "Roar, yhaaaahh, I feel things! I want to complain. It's painful! It's great to feel myself and complain instead of holding it in all the time. Wow! I feel great, Haah! Whoosh! Yeah! Wow!" Arny felt like joining her and began to make expressive sounds and complaints himself.

The woman then turned to the entire seminar group and said that she wanted everyone to be able to complain and feel what is troubling them instead of keeping everything inside. And she said that her agony was relieved when others expressed their suffering. Arny turned to the group as the other seminar participants began to complain and yell and express their feelings in sound and song. The woman was happy and quite relieved.

This woman realized that her process was not hers alone but belonged to the larger community.[1] Her individual process had a larger collective significance, that is, the desire of many people to express their deepest suffering and pain.

We notice how Arny follows the on-going feeling attitudes inside himself. First he pauses as he is touched by the woman's sense of death. He then follows his curiosity, which arises out of the belief in the wisdom of her process and the mysterious appearances of nature. (See Chapter Four on process oriented psychology). He follows her feedback and finally joins her as she makes sounds, and

---

[1] See Arny Mindell's *The Shaman's Body: A New Shamanism for Transforming Health, Relationships and the Community*, San Francisco: HarperCollins, 1993, pp. 44-45, 212-217.

complaints, feeling the collective significance of her process. His use of metaskills makes it possible to follow the flow of this woman's process.

The Practice of Psychotherapy

In psychotherapy, techniques and metaskills need one another. By themselves, metaskills suggest something like spirituality. We are reminded of compassionate individuals, religious leaders or gurus who identify with and state their metaskills explicitly. Metaskills are the central guide in their work. On the other hand, those people who identify mainly with their techniques are something like scientists.

The practice of psychotherapy, unlike religion or science, is the combination of the techniques and metaskills unique to each practitioner or therapeutic school. *Both* feelings and techniques bring psychotherapy to life.

In the above example, Arny uses his feelings in conjunction with other techniques such as amplification, movement, and auditory work to unfold the woman's process. Chapters Five through Twelve provide more examples of this interplay.

The Moon in the Water

The different feelings and attitudes that arise in any therapist's work are connected finally to the same source, to the underlying beliefs that the therapist, or therapeutic system, holds about life, human nature and therapy. Each metaskill is like one point of a crystal. Each facet shines in varying moments, yet all are attached to a central source. As C. G. Jung said, "... a man's philosophy of life ... guides the life of the therapist and shapes the spirit of his therapy."[1] Metaskills are the way this philosophy or

---

[1]C. G. Jung, "Psychotherapy and Philosophy of Life," *Collected Works,* Vol. 16, London: Routledge & Kegan Paul, 1954, p. 79.

belief reveals itself in practice. Therapy becomes as much a spiritual training for the therapist as it is for the client.

I am reminded again of the beautiful Zen image: the moon's reflection in the water. If we imagine fundamental beliefs as the moon in the sky, then metaskills are the reflection of the moon in the water. Metaskills reflect basic beliefs, but bring them down to earth as, hitting the surface of the water, they come to life in the river's continual flow. Our beliefs appear in living form through our metaskills.

Chapter Three

METASKILLS AND
SPIRITUAL PRACTICE

Metaskills can be cultivated and practiced in much the same way as other spiritual art forms. This cultivation of feeling attitudes is described eloquently in the training of Eastern spiritual traditions. These disciplines stress the *way* of performing any art form, martial art or meditation practice.

For example, when practicing the movement meditation *T'ai Chi*, the student must not perform the motions mechanically. Rather, the emphasis is on the way *T'ai Chi* is performed, the feeling behind it. Training focuses not only on exact motions but the ability to manifest the spiritual beliefs of *T'ai Chi* in each wave of the hand or brush of the leg. Thus, the way of performing the martial arts, arranging flowers or serving tea is a spiritual practice, requiring exact training, discipline, and spiritual development.

Indeed, the martial arts, which were primarily developed for warriorship, transformed during the peaceful Edo Period (1603-1867) into more spiritually oriented disciplines. This is reflected in the change of name from

43

bujutsu, meaning "martial skills or arts," to *budo*, the "martial way" or "martial path."

> In adopting a 'martial way' or 'path' during this peaceful era, the Japanese warrior was committing himself primarily to following a path aimed at spiritual development through martial training... Thus, the combat skill of ken-jutsu, the sword art, became kendo, the way of the sword; naginata-jutsu, the art of the halberd, became naginata-do, the way of the halberd, and so on.[1]

The therapist-in-training, too, is like the student of any art or spiritual discipline. She immerses herself in the thoughts, ideas and techniques of her school and, through training and practice, emerges as a fluid practitioner who manifests her deepest beliefs in living action.

Metaskills in Taoism

One of our greatest sources of information about metaskills can be found in Taoism. To follow the Tao—the flow of nature—the ancient Taoists required special feeling attitudes. The *Tao Te Ching*—the ancient poetic text written by Lao Tse, the legendary father of Taoism—does not specify techniques for following the Tao. Rather, this expressive book provides a rich description of the attitudes or qualities the sage must have to live in accordance with the Tao.

> In dwelling, be close to the land.
> In meditation, go deep in the heart.
> In dealing with others, be gentle and kind.
> In speech, be true.
> In ruling, be just.
> In business, be competent.

---

[1]H. Reid & M. Croucher, *The Fighting Arts,* New York: Simon & Schuster, 1983, p. 148.

In action, watch the timing.[1]

The manifestation of these attitudes was crucial to a Taoist way of life. The only way that we can grasp the knowledge of the sages is by observing their behavior. Indeed, it is most often the case that we discover feeling attitudes by observing *how* people go about their lives.

> Watchful, like men crossing a winter stream.
> Alert, like men aware of danger.
> Courteous, like visiting guests.
> Yielding, like ice about to melt.
> Simple, like uncarved blocks of wood.
> Hollow, like caves.
> Opaque, like muddy pools.[2]

The emphasis on the way the sage goes about life indicates that these attitudes were raised to the level of metaskills. The various attitudes—watchful, alert, courteous, yielding, simple, hollow, opaque—are metaskills reflecting the yielding philosophy of the Taoist who follows nature's changes. Many of these Taoist metaskills also appear in process oriented psychology and other therapeutic approaches whose roots lie in Taoist philosophy.

Techniques and Metaskills

The difference between technical skills and metaskills is well known in Eastern traditions. In his description of the martial arts, Peter Payne describes this difference.

> ... even an apparently correct movement without the spirit behind it will miss the mark in myriad subtle ways.

---

[1]Gia-Fu Feng & J. English, trans., *Tao Te Ching*, New York: Vintage, 1972, Chapter 8.
[2]Op. cit., Chapter 15.

A correction by the master may indicate this missing of the mark even if the external form is apparently correct.[1]

Payne describes the beauty of the master who allows his deep beliefs to guide and inspire his movements.

> The master stands in front of his students and allows the movements of his body to express his inner being through the form. The circular, rhythmic movements are like a river, a tree in motion, peaceful and silent as the sun rising, powerful as a stalking leopard, as empty of self-preoccupation as a blade of grass. And the students fumble their way through their empty simulations.[2]

The master focuses not only on the form but meditates on the way the form is filled with the spirit of the river, the tree or animal. This is the essence of the concept of metaskills; the focus on, and appreciation for, the basic feelings which pervade our actions.

Students of any discipline often look mechanical in comparison with their teachers. This is not necessarily due so much to a lack of skill as to the fact that the student may not yet be free enough with her or his form to allow the spiritual element behind the form to manifest.

We all know what it is like to listen to a great technical pianist or watch an excellent technical dancer. While the practitioner's work is technically amazing, something seems to be missing. The performance is not quite inspired; it lacks something essential that would really bring the art form to life. On the other hand, a dancer whose movements are filled with the feelings and inspiration behind his or her work makes us gasp and sigh as that original impulse is transferred to our bodies and minds.

Thomas Merton recounts that Chuang Tzu, Taoism's second most important writer, described and emphasized

---

[1]Peter Payne, *Martial Arts: The Spiritual Dimension*, London: Thames & Hudson 1981, p. 43.
[2]Ibid.

the *way* of carving wood as opposed to technical skills. The artist allows the "Tao" to speak through her as she works.

> ... we see that the accomplished craftsman does not simply proceed according to certain fixed rules and external standards. To do so is, of course, perfectly all right for the mediocre artisan. But the superior work of art proceeds from a hidden and spiritual principle which, in fasting, detachment, forgetfulness of results, and abandonment of all hope of profit, discovers precisely the tree that is waiting to have this particular work carved from it. In such a case, the artist works as though passively, and it is Tao that works in and through him.[1]

Merton reminds us of the significance of the attitudes of the craftsperson. Without these attitudes, we will perhaps never discover the "tree" that is waiting to be uncovered.

Like the techniques of the martial artist, dancer or musician, those of the therapist only make sense when they are inspired and infused with our underlying beliefs about life. Without this inspiration, techniques remain empty vessels lacking a sense of deeper significance.

Evolving Techniques

Not only is it important to manifest our deepest beliefs in practice, but it may actually be that our techniques grow and are created out of our basic attitudes. Ueshiba, the founder of aikido, says that techniques are not set in stone but must transform from moment to moment.

> The movements of aikido are extremely varied. Rather than following fixed forms, techniques are derived one after the other from a single basic principle. For this reason new techniques are still being born even now.

---

[1]T. Merton, *The Way of Chuang Tzu,* New York: New Directions, 1965, p. 30.

Infinite possibility hidden within the everyday—this is the distinguishing characteristic of aikido.[1]

Kenneth Kushner[2] tells a lovely story that illustrates the importance of allowing skills to spring forth from the well of belief. He describes his experience moving rocks at a monastery where he was training in kendo, Zen archery.

In this story, the Roshi instructed Kushner on how to move rocks by tipping them at a specific spot on the rock to discover the way in which the rocks wanted to move. Kushner went back to move more rocks, but his attempts failed. Some of the rocks were too big even to tip.

Later, the Roshi said that he had confused techniques (*ji*) with the underlying principles (*ri*). The principles are formless and unchanging. The techniques change from situation to situation. The Roshi told him that the specific manifestation of the principles would appear differently in each unique situation. The underlying principle was that each rock had its own way it naturally wanted to move. The person who wanted to move rocks had to be flexible enough to alter his techniques depending upon the nature of each rock!

I believe the Roshi was teaching us that we must not get stuck on any particular technique. Rather, techniques are created from the pool of principles and beliefs which guide our work. Remaining only with learned techniques makes our work stilted and uninspired. In the story of the rocks, the attitudes are the same: flexibility and the belief in the innate path of each rock. Yet, techniques transform from rock to rock.

---

[1] K. Ueshiba, *The Spirit of Aikido*, New York & Tokyo: Kodansha International 1987, p. 63.
[2] K. Kushner, *One Arrow, One Life: Zen, Archery and Daily Life*, London: Arkana, 1988, pp. 61-64.

In process work, Arny mentions that "no one set of techniques ... will fit every situation."[1] Rather, he tells us, the creativity of process work involves the development and transformation of our techniques in response to unique momentary signals and situations. The art of therapy becomes a creative and ever transforming act which is continually inspired by its deepest principles.

Dropping Technique

When one is really fluid in an art form, techniques become almost invisible. They fade into the background while the spirit of the Zen archer, the martial artist, the painter or the therapist remains. In fact, the "way" of shooting the arrow in Zen archery is not limited only to performing archery, but extends outward to every act of life. All of life becomes a reflection of this spiritual way, even when the bow has been put down.

Indeed, one of the goals of these disciplines is to ultimately drop the form and simply live in accordance with underlying principles. Metaskills continue while techniques become almost transparent. Taisen Deshimaru articulates this special development in the martial artist:

> Throughout this lifelong process, there is an inexorable shift in emphasis in the martial arts: from technique and strength of body in the beginning to exquisite intuition and a realization of spirit in the end. Master Morihei Ueshiba, the founder of modern aikido, realized the true potential of his art only after he turned seventy when he could no longer count on the power of his body.[2]

The spirit of the painter remains even when she has put her brush down. The awesome dancer is one whose

---

[1] *River's Way: The Process Science of the Dreambody,* London: Routledge & Kegan Paul, 1985, p. 25.

[2] T. Deshimaru, *The Zen Way to the Martial Arts: A Japanese Master Reveals the Secrets of the Samurai,* London: Century, 1982, p. 5.

technical skills become so much a part of her movement that they are transparent. The therapist who has trained thoroughly becomes a living example of the spiritual values of her particular therapeutic system. Her techniques become invisible. She is no longer "doing" therapy, or applying techniques, but living and manifesting her deepest beliefs in all that she does.

Spiritual Discipline

Ultimately the practice of any Eastern discipline—whether it be flower arranging, tea ceremonies, martial arts, poetry, meditation or painting—is a spiritual undertaking. [1]

> Although the Chinese have always insisted upon the perfection of techniques and design values, they never forgot that art was the vehicle for man's inmost thoughts and deepest inspiration. [2]

Each discipline is simply a path to spiritual attainment. Perhaps becoming a therapist, then, is also a spiritual path, if we learn to allow our underlying beliefs to surface through our work.

The learner on the path to becoming a therapist is, like the student of martial arts or meditation or Zen or Taoism, on a spiritual path. It is a path of learning, struggling and finally loosening ourselves from the grip of what we have learned in order to live in accordance with our basic feelings about life.

The therapist's techniques become transparent, infused with the spirit of her feelings and beliefs. She embraces the various feeling attitudes in her and allows them to shape, form and create her techniques as each situation unfolds.

---

[1] Thich Thien-an, *Zen Philosophy, Zen Practice,* Berkeley: Dharma Publishing and College of Oriental Studies, 1975, p. 131.

[2] G. Rowley, *Principles of Chinese Painting*, rev. ed., Princeton University Press, 1974, p. 79.

She becomes a model of someone who manifests her beliefs in living practice just as the moon's reflection rides the waves of the water.

Section II

PROCESS ORIENTED METASKILLS

Chapter Four

ROOTS OF PROCESS WORK

To understand the case examples that follow, you need to know something about the history and roots of process oriented psychology (process work).

History and Roots

When I arrived in Zurich, Switzerland in 1981 there was no "process oriented psychology." Rather, Arny was involved in something known as "dreambodywork."

Arny originally trained as a Jungian analyst. One of Jung's main tenets was the concept of teleology; that is, that events are striving toward a meaningful purpose or goal.[1] Jung used the image of the medieval alchemists who attempted to cook *prima materia*—or raw matter—until it turned to gold to describe the process of unfolding and appreciating the contents of the unconscious as they manifest in dreams.

While Jung applied this teleological concept mainly to dreams, Arny applied it as well in the 1960s to body experi-

---

[1]C. G. Jung , "The Soul and Death," *Structure and Dynamics of the Psyche*, Vol. 8, Princeton: Bollingen Series, 1969, p. 406.

ences.[1] In his work with dying patients, he discovered that physical symptoms, when amplified and allowed to unfold, mirrored dream images. The body and the imagery found in dreams were two channels of the same underlying process that was trying to come to our attention. Hence, the term "dreambody."

This discovery revealed that we do not only dream at night but are always dreaming through our spontaneous and unintentional signals. It is in the spontaneous occurrences of nature that we discover the solutions to our problems and the source of greater creativity. To follow this living "dreaming process" as it manifests from moment to moment Arny sought an impartial language that was not dependent upon such terms as body, matter or psyche, but which explained events in more neutral terms. He used information theory to define phenomena in terms of process, sensory oriented experiences, signals and channels. Hence the term "process" arose indicating the on-going flow of signals through various perceptual channels.[2]

The channels that seem to arise most frequently in practice include the visual channel, the auditory channel, the proprioceptive channel (referring to inner-body feelings), the kinesthetic or movement channel, the relationship channel (when we experience our process occurring in relationships), and the world channel (when we perceive our process as happening in relationship to the world around us). There are many other channels such as the olfactory (smell) channel and the spiritual channel. The therapist attempts to discover and unfold the dreaming

---

[1]Arny Mindell, *Dreambody: The Body's Role in Revealing the Self,* London & New York: Viking-Penguin, 1986, and *Working with the Dreaming Body*, London & New York: Viking-Penguin, 1986.

[2]Arny Mindell, *River's Way: The Process Science of the Dreambody,* London & New York: Viking-Penguin, 1985. See also Joseph Goodbread's *The Dreambody Toolkit*, New York: Viking-Penguin, 1987, for further discussion of basic process theory and methods.

process as it expresses itself in each evolving moment through these channels. Different therapists have a tendency to stress particular channels more than others.

Between 1981 and the present a group of students formed the Research Society for Process Oriented Psychology in Zurich. The terms "process oriented psychology" and "process work" came into use as more encompassing descriptions of the work that now focused on following the natural process whether it appeared in movement, body feelings, in interactions with others (relationships), or in groups. A training program evolved and process work has since been applied to individuals, couples, families and groups in various states of consciousness including comatose, extreme and psychotic states, and to large group conflict situations. Process work draws fundamentally on the tenets of Taoism, Zen, Alchemy, the work of C. G. Jung, shamanism, Native American traditions and modern physics. Process work has been applied all over the world and with individuals from many different cultural and ethnic backgrounds. Process work centers are now found in many countries including Australia, Russia, Poland, Japan, England and many other cities around the world.

Process work expands individual therapy because it has an ethical belief in connecting individual work to political, environmental and group work. It does not discriminate between sexes, races or classes, nor does it require that everyone become conscious.[1] Rather, those individuals who do not feel they are "sick" or in need of help are seen as city shadows,[2] who carry a message for the rest of society. Process work does not support the status quo or revolutionary forces inside ourselves or in our groups and communities but focuses rather on the representation of all

---

[1] See Arny Mindell, *City Shadows: Psychological Interventions in Psychiatry*, London & New York: Routledge & Kegan Paul, 1988.
[2] Ibid.

parties and the unraveling of the relationships among them.[1] It does not focus solely upon healing but upon the improvement of the quality of life as a whole.[2]

Process work investigates our known world and opens up to the unknown, the numinous and inexplicable elements of life that are the potential seeds of new life and creativity. It seeks to uncover the spiritual in our most mundane reality, in our most ordinary but spontaneous movements, in our greatest suffering through body symptoms or relationship problems, in the heat of an intense group conflict, or in the privacy of our internal dreams.

Process Work and Taoism

Taoism is a central building block behind process oriented beliefs.

The Chinese Taoist was concerned with observing the natural patterns and movement of nature and adjusting him- or herself to this flow.[3] The Taoist was fascinated by the "unending flux"[4] of nature. Taoists learned to adjust themselves to this winding course, or "Tao", and thereby lived harmoniously with its movement without questioning or trying to explain its manifestations. [5]

The process worker—like the ancient Chinese Taoist— tries to observe the spontaneous arrangements of nature and assist the client and herself to adjust to this changing flow.[6]

---

[1] See Arny Mindell, *Leader as Martial Artist: An Introduction to Deep Democracy*, San Francisco: HarperCollins, 1992.

[2] See Arny Mindell, *Working with the Dreaming Body*, London: Viking-Penguin, 1986 for examples.

[3] Blofeld, *Taoism, The Quest for Immortality*, London: Allen & Unwin, 1979, p. 10 and P. Rawson & L. Legeza, *The Chinese Philosophy of Time and Change*, London: Thames & Hudson, 1973, p. 11.

[4] Blofeld, op. cit., p. 5.

[5] Arny Mindell, *River's Way*, p. 90.

[6] Op. cit., p. 6.

She does not have a program as to what to do with a client, but allows nature to instruct her. She attempts to follow the Tao even though she is unable to know its exact origin, and even though it may flow into seemingly mysterious and unknown territories.[1] Like the Taoist, she assumes that everything the therapist or the client needs is already present in the spontaneous manifestations of nature. She must simply adjust, interact with and assist nature's path.

Arny, therefore, distinguishes the process worker from the traditional therapist as follows:

> For me, process work is a natural science. A process oriented psychologist studies and follows nature, while a therapist programs what he thinks should be happening. I don't believe in therapy because I don't know any more what is right for other people. ... I simply look to see what exactly is happening in the other person and what happens to me while he is reacting. I let the dreambody processes tell me what wants to happen and what to do next. That is the only pattern I follow. I do not press people. Their bodies and souls know better than I do.[2]

In this way, the process worker is a modern day Taoist who is fascinated by the "unending flux" of nature. A process oriented therapist seeks to unfold the spontaneous emergence of nature while knowing that it cannot be manipulated or hurried, only cradled and allowed to reveal itself in its own unique way and time.

As process work adapts to the changes in nature, it becomes somewhat mercurial. Its emphasis on the flow of nature in any moment requires that it take on characteristics of various known therapeutic forms. It resembles Freudian analysis in those moments when the client ponders early childhood. At another moment, process work resembles Gestalt therapy as, fascinated by a particular "dreamfigure,"

---

[1]Ibid.
[2]Arny Mindell, *Working with the Dreaming Body*, p. 9.

the client begins to speak as this character. Following the client's unconscious and perseverating movements may develop into a form of dance therapy. A process worker strives to follow the way nature changes and evolves. Therefore, any single session may include dance, Gestalt, word association, active imagination, bodywork and relationship work and any number of different methods.

Individual/World: An Example

The therapist discovers methods as they are spontaneously called for by the client's process. A group session may include whole group work, subgroup or relationship work, individual focus, bodywork, strong outer conflict or deeply introverted moments.

Before continuing with the discussion of the background of this work, I want to relate an example which was very meaningful to me. While this book focuses primarily on work with individuals, this situation occurred in a recent "worldwork" seminar involving three hundred people from thirty-five countries, and which focused on large group conflicts and multi-cultural tensions. This example demonstrates the flow among various channels and levels of group work (individual, relationship and group), and, most importantly, the emphasis on the social implications of individual work.[1]

---

[1]For further discussion of the connection between relationship work and group work, see Arny Mindell's *The Dreambody in Relationships* (1987) and *The Year One* (1989). Theory and examples of the way in which the various levels of individual, relationship and group work flow together and the theoretical and practical basis of process oriented group work may be found in *The Leader as Martial Artist* (1992). See Arny Mindell's soon to be published *Sitting in the Fire: The Politics of Awareness* for more on his views of the social implications of individual and relationship work and the social, cultural and political background to group work.

During one of the sessions, an African-American woman stood up and said that she wanted to talk about the racism she sensed in other group members. The focus therefore began on the group level. Yet, as the woman continued to speak she became short of breath. She said that she suffered from asthma and when she wanted to speak in public she was often plagued by asthmatic reactions as she attempted to talk.

She decided that she would like for a moment to explore her body symptoms. A switch happened momentarily as the focus turned toward her proprioceptive or internal body sensations. When Arny asked her how she experienced her asthma, she said it was like a tightening around her lungs. She expressed this by clenching her fists. As she went further with her experience of her fists, she began to punch the air, expressing her rage and anger at racial injustice. She finally dropped down to the floor in agony and sadness over the experience of being racially oppressed. As her lungs spontaneously began to relax, she turned once again to the group and began to talk poignantly and painfully about the agony of growing up as a black woman in the United States and how we must all become conscious of racism and create more tolerance in our world. The focus returned to the group and a discussion on racism evolved out of this woman's process. Her work awakened the entire group to the pervasiveness of racism, the agony it causes, and the way racism reveals itself subtlely in daily interactions.

This woman's individual work was intricately connected to collective and social reality. Her experience of her symptoms was not hers alone, but was inextricably tied to the attitudes of culture. If therapists are not aware of such connections, individual therapy may inadvertently ignore the reality of our world and its social issues.[1]

---

[1]See Arny Mindell's, *The Leader as Martial Artist* and *Sitting in the Fire: The Politics of Awareness* for a detailed discussion of metaskills for social, political and large group work. See also James Hillman and

The reader may have noticed how the process flowed from group work to individual work, from body symptoms to movement work and once again back to the large group focus. The process revealed its own unique path through various channels.

Arny's Taoism

As the years in Zurich went by, Arny and I became very close. We began to teach and work together and lead seminars in many countries around the world. I discovered more about myself and my feelings about my work as a teacher and therapist. I began to study process oriented therapists and search for this subtle feeling level of interaction which gave the work its passion and brought the deepest process oriented beliefs to life.

Arny seemed to use process oriented skills in an effortless way. Whether he was working with an individual with a chronic illness, someone in a psychotic state, someone lying in a coma or a couple in terrible conflict, his work was fluid and precise. The manifestation of process oriented beliefs was not limited to his therapeutic work but also permeated the way he lived.

I remember one of our first meetings. We had lunch together on the Lake of Zurich. We were about to cross a busy road to get to a cafe. Suddenly he was gone. Where did he go? I looked up and saw him already three quarters of the way across the road, dancing his way through the cars, taking all sorts of chances I would never take. While being kind and gentle, Arny seemed at the same time unfettered by the kinds of fears I had at that time. This man was truly mystifying! I also recall sitting together in a train

---

Michael Ventura's critique of therapy in *We've Had a Hundred Years of Psychotherapy and the World's Getting Worse*, San Francisco: HarperCollins, 1992.

one day and being disturbed by some rowdy teenagers who were looking at us. We were trying to prepare a seminar and feeling a bit lethargic about it. "Wonderful!" Arny said. "These teenagers are our teachers. Let's use them! We should learn from them. They are our allies!" I agreed wholeheartedly. We started preparing the seminar with new vigor and excitement as we brought more of these "rowdy" spirits into our work.

Process Oriented and Taoist Metaskills

In the following chapters I outline an array of metaskills that can be found in process oriented work, emphasizing the way they come alive and are interpreted through Arny's practice. These examples are, however, simply one way in which these Taoist beliefs find footing in practical application. Exactly how each individual therapist manifests these particular attitudes and blends them with technique is a matter of the conditions of the movement, personal style, as well as cultural and ethnic background. As far as I know, the metaskills that I present in the following chapters are cross-culturally applicable.

The metaskills described in this book are found in the work of individual therapists who share similar feelings about the nature of life. Anyone who believes that what happens in a given moment is potentially meaningful—if we become conscious of it and allow it to unfold—will notice many of these attitudes arising as she or he is working. Therapists who are guided by the unique client-and-therapist situation rather than predetermined programs, base their work on Taoism, the belief in nature and its changes. Each therapist, of course, will discover other metaskills that are not mentioned here.

Let me highlight, however, some central attitudes that arise in the process oriented therapist. For example, this therapist notices her *fluid* awareness which is able to follow and change in a moment's notice as nature itself winds its unique course, flowing between deeply internal states and outer ecstatic experiences, from individual to couple or group work. A Taoist notices her tendency to resist change and then the sudden *compassionate* opening up to all aspects of experience. She has moments of *detachment* which provide a necessary distance and perspective on life's events. The process worker is periodically *lazy* yet suddenly *jumps* up and catches the life force as it flickers in front of her. The sage can be as *playful* and *humorous* as she is *serious* and *respectful* and sometimes discovers a *beginner's mind* which, like a child, dives into life as if it were one mystery after another. She notices the tendency to think with discrimination like a *scientist.* At other moments she discovers a *shamanic* attitude that allows consensus reality to slip away and depths of mystery to teach her. Lastly, her *social* awareness realizes that individual work is intricately connected to our larger world.

While the examples that follow include moments of visual, verbal, kinesthetic, relationship and group work, those therapists who, for example, work primarily analytically with verbal discussions and imagery will manifest these metaskills in the way that she or he treats her clients and works with auditory and visual material. Body workers will demonstrate these metaskills in the way that he or she approaches, touches, and follows the client's body process. Movement therapists embody these metaskills in the way that they focus on movement.

Since I began this study of metaskills, the term has become widely accepted in the process work community. Arny applied it in *The Leader as Martial Artist: An Introduction to Deep Democracy* and in his *Sitting in the Fire: The Politics of Awareness,* which outline not only the *skills*, but also the *metaskills* we need to work with large group and conflict situations. What future applications of metaskills will be discovered remains a challenge to us all.

The following chapters present case examples of work primarily with individuals (except for Chapter Eleven, which focuses on a group of children) drawn from public seminars whose themes included introduction to process work, process work with chronic body symptoms, process oriented movement work, and process work with children. The seminars took place in East Asia, Western Europe and the United States. Volunteers worked with Arny in the center of the seminar group as the rest of the participants look on. Each case was transcribed verbatim from video-taped recordings. The material is altered only to maintain confidentiality. Although these examples deal with short term therapy, the metaskills which will be discussed arise as well in long-term work. A more detailed description of metaskills in long-term therapy is a further research area.

These chapters offer a living view into the world of metaskills. Each case illustrates many different metaskills just as feelings and moods arise continually in the therapist as she is working. I highlight particular metaskills and describe them in the discussions that follow each case. I amplify these metaskills through analogies to the martial arts, Zen, Taoism, Chinese painting, the work of Carlos Castaneda and modern physics.

Chapter Five

COMPASSION

A really good therapist is often described by her clients as compassionate or empathetic. She or he has a special feeling capacity that makes it possible to understand and feel into the world of the client. Compassion is also an important quality in many spiritual traditions.

All of us know how much better we feel around someone who is really compassionate and attentive to us. This feeling can be so significant that its presence, or the lack of it, may define a very good or a very bad experience with someone. And each of us knows what it is like to be compassionate to ourselves instead of turning away from ourselves in distrust or dislike.

In process oriented terms, compassion is differentiated in a very specific way which involves embracing *all* of the different aspects of ourselves. Before describing this meta-skill and how we can use it both in therapy and everyday life, let's take a look at an example from one of our seminars in an East Asian country. The work was translated from the man's native language into English.

SHIVERING

A man about 20 years old came forward in the seminar. He said that he had had neurological damage at birth and that he wanted to explore one of his body symptoms. He spoke in a slow, impaired voice, and his thumbs were curled in. He said that he had extreme tremors whenever he was tense and unable to relax. He was unable to alleviate the tremors medically. He said that he was feeling the tremors just now in his arms. He and Arny began to work on his body experiences as the rest of the group looked on.

Arny said that it must be dreadful not to be able to relax and then asked the man if he would like to investigate what the tremors could be about. The man giggled and faltered. Arny said that he could understand the man's hesitation, yet perhaps this troublesome symptom could teach him something useful about his life. The man became interested and agreed excitedly to find out more about his shivering.

Arny encouraged him to amplify or intensify the experience of shivering by allowing the trembling to spread through his arms to the rest of his body. Soon the man was shaking all over.

Arny then asked if the man could cause Arny to shake. That is, instead of the man's experiencing himself as the victim of the shaking, he would now become the symptom-creator and cause Arny to shiver. The man paused, approached Arny, shyly reached out and started to shake Arny from the shoulders, down Arny's arms to his hands. The man's own shaking stopped.[1]

"What is it you are doing to me?" Arny asked.

The man paused, searching for words to express the feelings that were building up. Suddenly with great emotion and pain the man cried, "I want to convey that I'm suffering!!!"

---

[1]See the section in Chapter 10 called "The Symptom Creator" for further discussion of why the man's shaking stopped at this moment.

Arny replied, "Yes, go on and say everything that you feel."

As the man started to push Arny away slightly, he shrieked in agony, "Wake up! There's pain here!!!" The man's suffering became vivid and tangible to everyone in the group. He cried. Arny and he paused together for this heart-wrenching moment.

After some time Arny asked the man if he would like to go back to the moment when his movements turned into a slight push. The man began to push Arny slightly again and then gave Arny a big push. As Arny stumbled to the other side of the room, the man said, "Get out of my way!!"

Arny turned and said, "Yes! You hate all the pressure that has been put on you because of being a differently-abled person."

The man nodded and cried. They stood together for a moment.

Arny then asked if the man would like to experiment once again with his energetic push to find out more about it. The man hesitated briefly and then experimented again with forcefully pushing Arny. After a few trials, the man began to smile. He was enjoying his new found strength. Arny said, "You shouldn't sit passively back, it's good to push things out of the way sometimes!" and explained, "You can't relax because you need to use all this pushing energy in your everyday life."

Arny mirrored the man's pushing movements so the man could imagine how he could use this force in everyday life. The man joined him in the pushing. Arny spoke in the rhythm of their movements and said, "Yes, make the motions...and...as you move...think how you could use...this in everyday life."

Suddenly, the man said, "I want to use this energy to be a politician!"

Arny stopped dead in his tracks. "Wow!" Arny said. "Someone who knows what it is to feel and suffer and live with physical disabilities is the right politician. We could all use someone like that, someone who can speak from the heart!"

The man agreed and said that he very much wanted to be able to speak out about his and other people's suffering but was quite shy. Arny told him "I like the shy side of you and also love your powerfulness and the politician in you. We need it!"

The man looked at Arny knowingly and relieved. He contemplated the message from his symptoms for a moment silently. Arny and the man made little bows to one another and the man sat back down.

✳✳✳✳✳

Compassion in Process Work

Before discussing this case, let's define compassion in process oriented terms. Process work defines compassion as nurturing, caring for, and attending to those parts of ourselves that we like and identify with while *attending equally to* and appreciating those parts that we do not like, that we disavow and that are far from our identity. Further, compassion involves helping all of these parts to unfold and reveal their essential nature and meaning. Therefore, compassion means attending to all the aspects of our experience and consciously allowing each to unfold.

This definition of compassion grows out of process work theory, which states that it is only when all of the parts of ourselves, our relationships or groups, are represented that our individual, couple or group system works wisely.[1] This belief develops very specific metaskills in the therapist who trusts and believes in the inner wisdom of the individual and the process that is trying to unravel—whether aspects of that process appear as a "monster," a chronic symptom, an addiction, an extreme state or a wild group meeting. It is

---

[1]Arny Mindell, *The Year One*, New York & London: Penguin, 1989, p. 61.

only when this man's shyness *as well as his power* is represented consciously that his process makes sense and acts intelligently.

The Technology of Compassion

Process oriented compassion requires not only a special feeling ability of openness to our different experiences, but also a scientific ability which can discover those experiences of which we are not normally aware. Typically, we notice those aspects of our experience that are close to the way we identify ourselves (primary process) and do not take note of those experiences or signals that are further away from our identity (secondary processes). These latter signals are unintentional and may be disturbing. Secondary experiences may occur, for example, in spontaneous and incomplete motions (such as facial tics, or tripping while walking down the street), body symptoms, relationship difficulties, dream images, or environmental synchronicities (such as the sudden squawking of birds in a meaningful moment). Secondary phenomena are unknown mysteries awaiting unfolding. They are incongruent with our momentary identities. If we aren't aware of the distinction between primary and secondary processes, we may support only the primary process of ourselves or our clients and disavow other aspects which are trying to get our attention.

In the case example, Arny appreciates the man's primary process. He is shy and has a desire to relax. Arny also notices and attends to the man's secondary experiences— his disturbing body symptoms and movements. A compassionate attitude opens us up to this man's symptoms, imagining that they may be the door to new worlds, solutions and unlived dreams.

Why does process work define compassion in this way? It is easy enough for us to love the parts of ourselves that we like but how many of us really appreciate those aspects of ourselves that we do not want to have? True love is all-encompassing: it focuses attentively on all parts of ourselves. All of us have felt neglected at one time or another. While this reflects an outer reality that must be addressed, part of this feeling may have to do with our inability to nurture the different sides of ourselves, particularly to embrace those unusual or spontaneous aspects of our experience that could lead to greater creativity and wisdom.

Because our normal minds have a tendency to block out and disavow experiences that do not go along with our identities, these "secondary" elements of our process rarely receive any attention or focus. Even the most well-meaning therapist may filter out aspects of a client's process. Meditation or therapeutic practices that concentrate on the continuum of awareness, for example, may skip over flickering secondary phenomena if the therapist does not help the person return to and focus on them. Therapeutic systems which focus on visual material may miss the flickering signals of inner-body experiences. Many of us spend the day focusing on visual or auditory aspects of our experience and block out unusual movement signals or disturbing relationship experiences.

One of the reasons that we tend to neglect secondary experiences is because of the "edge." In process theory, the edge is the boundary between our known world and the unknown. It occurs in the moment when something new and unknown arises, and we find ourselves faltering and falling back into our known identity. Sometimes people giggle, hesitate or become shy at the edge as new experiences begin to emerge. At the edge, a compassionate therapist follows the individual's awareness. If the client wants to go over the edge into new territory, then that is the direction to go. If the client stays at the edge, the therapist can find out more about the inhibitions to going over that edge. Perhaps the client simply needs encouragement to step out of ordinary time and follow something that is mysterious. In our example, the edge appears when the man gets close to his experience of shivering. Arny notices the man's hesitation but then the man's excitement to explore this unknown experience takes over.

The metaskill of compassion requires, in addition to feeling, accuracy in awareness. We need a technology of compassion that allows us to differentiate and value all sides of nature. It requires awareness of the edge and the careful and loving appreciation for this dynamic moment. As we discover this feeling attitude inside ourselves, we use it consciously to notice and unfold all of the various aspects of our client's lives. In this way, compassion becomes a metaskill.

Deep Democracy

There are many ways to describe the metaskill of compassion. Arny's term *deep democracy*[1] grew out of large group work. It describes the facilitator's openness to, and appreciation for, all parts of a group. It means allowing all the different sides of the group to emerge and communicate with one another; the authority, the rebel, the fearful and silent parts all have a forum for their expression.[2]

A deeply democratic attitude towards ourselves means supporting all of our various sides. Instead of relying on the traditional approach of "majority rule,"[3] which favors only our identity or primary process, we open up to secondary, disavowed experiences. But who is really democratic, especially when we consider our inner worlds which are most often run by tyrannical forces that sit upon our less desirable parts? How many of us are truly open to all sides

---

[1] In his book, *The Leader as Martial Artist*, 1991, Arny discusses the concept of deep democracy in great detail. See especially pp. 5-6 and pp. 148-160.

[2] Op. cit., Chapters 3 and 4.

[3] From a lecture of Arny's on deep democracy, 1990.

of ourselves? How many of us notice such spontaneous motions as tripping slightly as we walk, or the scratchiness of our voice, disturbing body feelings, painful body symptoms, or troublesome relationship issues? [1]

In process oriented work with comatose patients, compassion or deep democracy means remembering the statements the person made about life and death before lapsing into the coma, and also following any unusual body signals and sounds from the comatose state.[2] Process work with chronic symptoms means appreciating and understanding the medical causes for symptoms as well as valuing and exploring the potential meaning inside these somatic experiences.

Eastern Traditions

The early Taoists were deep democrats of their times. They embraced all parts of nature equally.

> A dedicated Taoist is one who seeks to live as closely in accord as possible with nature's ways, recognition of their fitness, and perception that all of them are 'good' in the sense of being essential to the pattern as a whole. Depart from them and chaos and destruction loom.[3]

Zen philosophy teaches us that our attitudes can transform ordinary or unusual aspects of nature into beauty.

> ... from the Zen point of view, which is also the Japanese way of feeling, a thing, however misshaped, is

---

[1] Is it possible to develop this kind of compassion in ourselves? Amy has said that having compassion toward your body experiences is often much easier if you live in, or have access to a community which supports the investigation and expression of the different parts of yourself.

[2] See Amy Mindell, *Coma: The Dreambody Near Death,* London & New York: Viking-Penguin, 1994, for detailed descriptions of work with comatose patients.

[3] J. Blofeld, op.cit., p. 10.

perfect and artistic in its being misshaped. What is needed here to make an imperfection perfect is the presence of the artist's spiritual love for the object—a love which is above egotism but which issues from Great Spirit.[1]

Another closely related concept to process oriented compassion is "equanimity" in Buddhist Vipassana meditation. Equanimity, in this context, refers to a neutral focus; the ability to accept whatever nature is pointing to in a given moment with a neutral and fair heart.[2]

Riding the Horse Backwards

Elsewhere, Arny and I have described compassion as "riding the horse backwards."[3] What does this mean? Opening up to those parts of ourselves that we do not identify with, following the irrational or mysterious elements of our processes, is like turning our minds inside out. Our normal instinct and training tell us to alleviate body symptoms, to forget about our troubling neighbors, to clean the air of distractions, to ignore spontaneous movement signals, to push out the rebel, or to ignore the tiny child who is asking for attention inside of us. Who in their right mind would amplify a body symptom? Who dares ride the horse backwards?

The Heyoke figure in Native American stories rides the horse backwards.[4] Instead of riding forwards like everyone else, this trickster figure rides backwards on his horse. The process worker and anyone who follows the spontaneous

---

[1] D. T. Suzuki, *The Awakening of Zen*, Boston: Shambhala, 1987, p. 60. Thanks to Carl Mindell for having pointed out this similarity between equanimity and process oriented compassion.

[2] J. Goldstein, *The Experience of Insight: A Simple and Direct Guide to Buddhist Meditation*, Boulder: Shambhala, 1976, pp. 146-147.

[3] Mindell & Mindell, op. cit., Chapter 1.

[4] Ibid.

expressions of nature also goes backwards—noticing and appreciating the unusual, disavowed aspects that we tend to ignore, viewing them as the potential seeds of meaningful experiences. In this moment we are like advocates for the disavowed whose voices are rarely heard. Indeed, it is just in the unknown, secondary experiences that we discover the solutions to our problems.[1]

Returning to the man in our case example, by following his shaking we discover the pain and suffering involved in his disability and a tremendous force that wanted to push out and become a politician. Arny does not assume that the man's shivers result solely from his neurological difficulties and he avoids interpreting these signals. He rides the horse backwards by compassionately letting the experience of shivering unfold in its own unique way.

I remember another example of a woman who suffered from migraine headaches. She had had migraines all her life. Although she took medication to control the pain, they were a constant plague to her. A compassionate attitude says, why not explore what message might be lying behind these symptoms, since she is already doing everything she can medically to ease the pain? Perhaps these persistent symptoms are the beginning of a mystery that is attempting to unfold.

When she amplified the blurring of vision and sound that accompanied the migraine, she became dizzy and then began to shake and twitch. Suddenly she said, "I feel like an old crazy prophet roaming the streets of Jerusalem!"

A prophet was trying to come out of her through her symptoms! Who could have known this in advance?

The process worker does not make an hypothesis about where signals come from—unless the client brings this up spontaneously—but instead joins the mysterious flow of events and allows experience to explain itself.

---

[1] Amy Mindell, *Working with the Dreaming Body*, p. 84.

Courage and the Warrior

What else does it take to open up to disavowed aspects of ourselves and others? I think it requires something like the courage of a warrior who can shift focus from the momentary identity of ourselves, a client, or group to something that lies outside that known world. It is a courageous leap to step into the unknown. Even a very compassionate therapist may lack the courage or inner strength to negotiate a shift in worlds.

Courage is implied when the Yaqui Indian shaman Don Juan in Carlos Castenada's writings urges us unsentimentally to notice our secondary, mysterious processes. This involves a temporary break with culture, which is hard, and yet may bring relief to the suffering of our primary identity.

When the man in the example begins to cry just after he has pushed, Arny respects the man's sadness about his situation. Yet Arny also feels that it might be even more useful and a greater relief to the man if he gains access to his strength and discovers what the strong push aimed to achieve. It takes courage to remain at this powerful moment and discover more about the unknown pushing motions. When the man decides to explore his movements even further, we discover that what seemed at first to be sadness over his situation was actually the beginning of his desire to be a politician.

The metaskill of compassion reminds us to notice those aspects of our experience which we identify with and those aspects which we do not identify with, to help the latter as well as the former to unfold—to follow the river's flow, to open up to life's mysteries and to join in the unfolding of its unpredictable and potentially meaningful events.

Chapter Six

RECYCLING

The metaskill of compassion requires that we focus on unusual and unwanted experience and don't simply toss it in the garbage. Rather, we notice it, pick it up and, like the medieval alchemist, cook it until its gold or secret is revealed. Compassion leads us to become modern-day ecologists[1] and recycle not only plastics and paper but also experiences we would normally discard!

As ecologists we discover the spiritual in the mundane. We find gems in seemingly insignificant, tiny signals. Each disturbance, shift of posture or accidental stumble is potentially full of meaning and wisdom. Whether working with an individual, a couple or a group, a therapist takes nothing for granted. She or he becomes a recycler of those aspects of our individual and collective lives that we tend to ignore.

As you read the following example, see if you can discover the aspect of nature that we would tend to overlook, throw away, or take for granted. After the example,

---

[1]The use of the concept of ecology in individual and group work can be found in Arny's *The Year One*.

we will look at the metaskill of recycling and the tools
necessary to help these experiences unfold.

ORCHID POWER!

A 90-year-old woman, Margaret, says that she would like
to work on herself. She sits in her chair facing Arny.

> M (in a determined voice): I made a commitment
>   to live for another decade, (pause) wonderful
>   what all is happening.
> A: Commitment to live because ...?
> M: I have work to do and lots of joy in doing it.
> A: What work?
> M: Serving, growing, becoming.
> A: You mentioned serving first.
> M: I feel needed and I like that, like it matters
>   whether I'm alive or not ... (pause)
> A: To whom?
> M: Myself. (She looks down and pauses)
> A: And others?
> M: Yes. (pause) I like to feel we are learning and
>   growing together and I've spent a lot of time
>   doing that.
> A: What else?
> M: Not a whole lot else (pause as she looks down
>   for a moment).

What do you notice? If you *do not take anything for
granted*, what would you notice? Yes, the tiny signal that
we would tend to overlook is the *pause* in Margaret's
speaking. It is mysterious because it is not consistent or
congruent with her intended, primary process discussion
about life. We do not readily understand this signal; it is so
subtle, it would be easy to take it for granted. Let us see,
however, what happens when this signal is appreciated and
allowed to unfold.

A: I notice pauses between sentences now and then.

M: Why? Do you like them? What do they say to you? I'm not running as fast. I used to have to be first ...

A: So now perhaps we could be last and see what happens in the pause.

M: (Considering) What happens in the pause ... (She stops for a moment. Arny and the woman look down silently. She is quiet for a moment, breathes deeply, seems to be very internal and says quietly) Awareness ... Beingness ... whatever is happening ... (and then excitedly) Taking time to smell the flowers!

A: Oh! Let's smell the flowers together.

M: (She pauses for a moment, eyes closed, then looks up and says almost dreamily) Orchids.

A: Can you smell them?

M: (With a faint smile) Yes, I can smell them and see them blooming in my head.

A: You see them, smell them, they are blooming in your head ... what do they move like, the orchids?

M: They stretch out and are very gentle and the colors are soft and bright. (She begins to make motions outward with one of her hands)

A: Could you show me with both arms? Could we stand up for a moment?

M: (They stand up and Margaret begins to move her arms very softly and slowly) They are very gentle.

A: Go ahead and be a gentle orchid. (She moves beautifully, gently, as if doing a very slow and graceful *t'ai chi*.)

M: The breeze makes them move. (Margaret hesitates for a moment and says) But I don't always want to be a gentle orchid!

A: You can be whatever you want.

M: (Reconsidering) I think I'll stay that way for now. (She begins to move again as she speaks) I used to always have to be out there doing it, in front. It's not important now. (Giggling and reconsidering) Well not very important now!

A: You're an honest orchid! (Everyone in the group laughs and admires her honesty and the beautiful movements she is making.)

M: (Turning to Arny) Hey, how did we get off on orchids? You know, I went to a wedding and there were masses and masses of orchids. So beautiful!

A: Yes, masses of them.

M: (Sitting once again) What are we going to do with it? I really have a picture of all those I saw this morning. I've had a very long and exciting life. I believe in the commitment I made and I very much want to live, and I have news for you, I'm going to!

A: There are all sorts of ways to live. Was that the orchid that just spoke or another part?

M: (Giggling shyly) That was the stronger part of me. But you know, although the orchids look delicate, they are actually very hearty. They're not like scrawny old plants dead on the vine.

A: You have orchid power!

M: Orchid power! I like that!

The blooming orchids grow out of the subtle pauses in Margaret's speech. It is literally in the space, in the pauses, in the seemingly insignificant signals and gestures where the numinous, dreaming process presents itself!

Zen: Spirit in the Mundane

The recycling therapist is a true Zen adept who appreciates even the most minute aspects of nature.

> ... with Zen people nothing was trivial, everything, including even the smallest incidents of our daily experience, was a matter of grave concern; for even the lifting of a finger, or the opening of the mouth, the eyebrow raised, or the shepherd singing was pregnant with Zen.[1]

I sometimes describe this metaskill as the *lover of the absurd*. That is, appreciating and unfolding those aspects of experience that ordinarily seem *absurd* or have no *apparent* meaning. Arny describes this feeling as follows:

> Like an alchemist, I am a believer in nature and a spiritual person. The hundreds of people I have encountered in extreme states have shown me that hidden in the most impossible or absurd conditions is something wondrous. I see human nature as a deity, for in the most confusing chaos one finds the seeds of creation.[2]

Beginner's Mind

To notice even these seemingly insignificant aspects of experience, we may need a Zen attitude called *beginner's mind*. The beginner's mind is a mind—or perhaps heart—that is open and unbiased. It is not shaded by knowledge but is free and spontaneous enough to follow what we normally forget or overlook. Shunryu Suzuki reminds us, "If your mind is empty, it is always ready for anything; it is open to everything. In the beginner's mind there are many possibilities; in the expert's mind there are few."[3]

---

[1]Blofeld, op. cit., p. 58.
[2]Arny Mindell, *Coma: The Dreambody Near Death*, p. 53.
[3]Suzuki, op. cit., p. 21.

This beginner's mind allows us to appreciate and notice seemingly inconsequential events. Suzuki likens this attitude to compassion. "When your mind is compassionate, it is boundless."[1] Naturally, we cannot program ourselves to have this beginner's mind, yet anyone who believes in the flow of nature will discover this feeling at various times arising spontaneously as a sense of curiosity about the absurd. We are then free to explore the multiple and mysterious manifestations of life. In that moment, we open up to the most "insignificant" of events—we give grounding to our desire to recycle and unravel our deepest experiences and dreams.

Primary Process Descriptions of Secondary Phenomena

One of the pitfalls which cloud the beginner's mind is the common tendency of our primary process, or identity, to give static labels to unusual and unknown experiences. Such names as "tremors" (as in Chapter Five), "shyness," "evil," "bad spirits," "migraines" or "pauses" are the way our ordinary consciousness defines, organizes and solidifies secondary phenomena. This tendency is quite natural, and yet these names are merely fixed labels for signals that are in the middle of transformation. Labeling experience is like taking a picture of a car in motion. The picture can never explain or show where the car is going.[2]

Lao Tse puts this another way. "The Tao which can be told is not the eternal Tao."[3] Once we name the Tao, we try to solidify it. But we must not mistake this name for the Tao itself. The Tao is the ongoing flow of process. The Taoist oracle, the *I Ching*,[4] describes this flow and the

---

[1]Op. cit., p. 22.
[2]See Arny Mindell's, *River's Way*, Chapter 2 for more on this.
[3]Feng & English, op. cit., Chapter 1.
[4]See Richard Wilhelm's translation, London: Routledge & Kegan Paul, 1983.

direction of the Tao in a given moment in the form of hexagrams or pictures with "moving lines." These lines indicate that change is inherent in any picture or experience. Process work focuses on this "moving line," the dynamic, flowing aspect of nature, rather than the stationary hexagram.[1]

A process worker, therefore, focuses on the process which is *in potentia*, which flickers momentarily, which we cannot understand, which disturbs or disrupts our identities. In the example, it is the pause which, when unfolded with a beginner's mind, flows into the experience of the orchids. The process worker catches the movement inside of what seems to be a static state and helps it naturally unfold. We focus therefore on the movement and change inherent in our dreaming process.

Compassion and Experience

Once we notice things that we would normally take for granted, what then? What does it mean to understand these events? This leads us to another Buddhist teaching. We cannot understand events by standing outside and giving them all sorts of names and interpretations. Instead, D. T. Suzuki says, we must get into the current of experience and from this dynamic viewpoint allow events to explain themselves.[2] We cannot tell what the pauses in Margaret's speech are about if we look at them solely from a distance. It is through their unfolding that they explain themselves to us.

Whether working with body symptoms, addictions, relationship troubles, or group conflicts, the process worker does not remain with her initial knowledge about these states but attempts to get into the river of experience and

---

[1]From Arny Mindell's lecture on Taoism, Hawaii, 1989.

[2]D. T. Suzuki, *Zen and Japanese Culture*, Princeton University Press, 1973, pp. 23-24.

understand them from the inside out. She knows that once processes begin to unravel they reveal new worlds, stories, solutions and creative potential that could not have been predicted ahead of time. She differentiates elements of experience and then stands back humbly, allowing the process itself to be her teacher and guide.

Recycling Tools

The metaskill of recycling reflects an open and inquisitive attitude toward nature, especially those aspects we tend to ignore or throw away. A recycling therapist uses her interest in all aspects of life to notice subtle, almost imperceptible, secondary experiences such as hesitations in speech, incomplete gestures, incomprehensible postures, strange sounds, sudden visions, unusual body feelings or spontaneous movements. All of us know that it is no longer tenable to continually throw away garbage without recycling. Now we apply this concept to our inner lives, to our relationships and group experiences.

But what do we do once we notice secondary experiences? Noticing these signals is the beginning, but the Tao becomes meaningful only when we use our awareness to unfold its contents. To discover the divine in reality the recycling therapist needs both her feeling attitude toward events and also tools to help structure and unfold experiences. The main tools for unfolding the elements of any process are amplification and channel changing.

Amplification

The alchemists took raw materials, put them in a pot and cooked them in the hope that they would turn into gold. They used various processes to do this but it was their special attitudes of attention and reverence that created the atmosphere in which basic material could transform.[1]

The process worker, like the alchemists, cares for and "cooks" spontaneous events by focusing on them and amplifying their signals. Amplification means following and intensifying a signal in the particular sensory oriented channel in which it appears so that its full message can emerge.

The idea of amplification is one that has long been known and appreciated in the East. On our first trip to Japan, we learned a great lesson from watching Japanese flower arranging. The artist tries to discern the natural spirit and movement tendency within the flowers and leaves. Then, subtly and skillfully, the artist follows this movement, assisting nature in its natural direction. The rocks and sculptures of Japanese gardens are a beautiful example of an artist's following nature's inherent tendencies. Similarly, the process worker attempts to discover the natural tendency of unknown and mysterious signals and follow their unique course.

By amplifying spontaneous events and allowing them to naturally unfold, we discover that our experiences are not haphazard and random but glimpses of a larger dreaming process from which they arise. We might begin with a small, seemingly insignificant signal and, as it unfolds, suddenly discover our dreams from the night before, mythic stories or spiritual experiences that are trying to come to our attention. Spontaneous events are not chaotic but have an inherent logic of their own.[2]

---

[1]For further discussion of alchemy and process work see Arny Mindell, *River's Way*, 1985, pp. 118-140.

[2]Op. cit., p. 60.

Channels

Amplifying a signal means discovering the channel in which the signal is occurring and then intensifying that experience. If a signal occurs in the visual channel, that signal can be amplified by seeing the vision more clearly, looking closely at the colors, shapes and forms, or perhaps enlarging the picture. Auditory experiences can be amplified by listening to the sounds more closely. If the sound is a voice, we can determine whether it is a male or a female voice. Amplification of spontaneous movements could include increasing the spatial expression of that movement or doing it in slow motion. A body sensation felt in one part of the body could be amplified by increasing this feeling momentarily to include the whole body.

In which channel does the work with Margaret begin? The pauses seem to occur in the proprioceptive (body feeling) channel as she looks down and apparently is feeling something. Therefore, amplification means asking her to notice what happens as she focuses on her inner-body feelings. She begins to recycle this unknown signal as she focuses compassionately upon it.

Channel Changing

Once you have amplified a given signal in its channel, you may discover another method that nature has for amplifying information. Channel changing. Have you ever noticed moments when you are focusing on a sound and you suddenly change channels and notice what you are feeling in your body? To fully experience something, it is helpful to consciously change channels and help processes express themselves more fully. If you are seeing something, why not translate that picture into inner-body feelings? How about expressing this body feeling in movement and sound?

If you are hearing a discussion, try to see a picture of the people who are talking.[1]

In the example above, the work begins proprioceptively. The channels begin to change as Margaret starts to *smell* the orchids and then *sees* them. She uses the kinesthetic channel as she begins to *move* like these beautiful orchids and imagines how to integrate this experience into everyday life. Through amplification and channel changing she discovers the larger dreaming process peeping through her pauses.

Changing States

To recycle secondary information, the therapist will need to "stop the world" as Don Juan says.[2] This means dropping out of consensus reality temporarily. When we step out of our ordinary identities, we find ourselves in *altered* states of consciousness in which new information can emerge.[3]

Our ordinary consciousness wants to hold onto what is known. Yet, the ability to leave the world of our ordinary identity for a moment may finally be of greater service to the whole person or group. In Margaret's work, the world stops in the moment when she focuses on her pauses. Arny noticed how Margaret lowered her eyes as she paused and helped her follow this altered state.

Learning to ride the waves of altered states is crucial in working with people in comas and extremely withdrawn states. The therapist is required to use communication methods that interact directly with these individuals in

---

[1]See Arny Mindell, *Working on Yourself Alone*, 1989, Chapters 4-8 for more on channel changes.

[2]Carlos Castaneda, *Journey to Ixtlan*, London: Penguin, 1974, p. 267.

[3]See Arny Mindell, *The Shaman's Body: A New Shamanism for Transforming Health, Relationships, and the Community*, San Francisco: Harper, 1993, for a detailed discussion of the interface between process work and the teachings of Don Juan.

altered states of consciousness. This is in contrast to asking these individuals to adapt to our reality and means of communicating. The therapist's ability to do this determines whether the client feels related to or isolated. Arny says:

> ... many people going through these altered states need our help to realize their total selves. Indeed, they want intimate communication. Many prefer it to ordinary loving compassion. For without it, a special moment can be missed as the mind spins wildly in a turbulent river flowing to the sea.[1]

Once we worked with a man in a comatose state who was close to death and drowning of pneumonia.[2] Instead of assuming that his rasping was due only to the fluid in his lungs, and after necessary medical interventions, we amplified the noises he was making. We imitated his sounds and added more sounds. The man began to respond to us in sound and we started a communication system. Eventually, he came out of his coma and began to really rasp and sputter and from this noise he began to sing children's songs. His lungs cleared and he became a conductor who guided us in singing along with him! His rasping was the beginning of a festive event! During the next day he expressed many loving feelings which he was otherwise shy about and died peacefully that night.

Not Taking Your Own Signals for Granted

Ecology also means that the therapist does not take her own signals for granted. Many therapists have been trained not to bring in their own processes while working. This can be important particularly if a therapist has not been trained to carefully follow the feedback of the client. Yet modern

---

[1] See *Coma: The Dreambody Near* Death, p. 102.
[2] Ibid.

developments in psychotherapy and physics remind us that we are an intricate part of the field we are living in.

Perceiving and bringing in your signals means, in part, seeing yourself as a channel for the larger dreaming field that is trying to express itself.[1] This is the essence of field theory, which tells us that it is difficult to know where we as individuals begin and where we end. Anything happening in a particular field or environment is part of a common dreaming process expressing itself. We can no longer separate me from you but rather must concentrate on the expression of the dreaming process wherever it appears.

Not taking your own signals for granted can have very important effects. I remember a therapist once working with a woman who had a stomach cramp. She wanted the therapist to touch her stomach but the therapist noticed that she was unable to do so. She noticed her own hesitations and told this to her client. Shortly thereafter the woman told of numerous instances where she had been intruded upon or violated by members of the medical profession. Had the therapist ignored her own reactions, she would have repeated this intrusion. In this case, the therapist gently brought in her own feelings, the client began to tell her story and together they went further into the process as the client directed what to do.

Of course, each therapist has to decide when it is and is not useful to bring his or her own signals into the work. This depends very much on individual circumstances and the style of the therapist. If the therapist does bring in her own experiences, it is crucial that she watch closely for the feedback of the client and adjusts to this feedback.

Ecology in Group Work

The concept of ecology as applied to group work means focusing not only on those aspects of group and community

---

[1]Amy Mindell, *River's Way*, p. 55.

life that the group identifies with, but also on those aspects we tend to ignore—that do not go along with the group's identity—and helping these aspects come forward as well. For example, a modern or new age organization, committed to non-hierarchical structure, may "throw out" or disregard the role of the individual in the group who wants to take power and lead. Ecology in this case might mean creatively representing this hierarchical voice and allowing it to communicate with all of the other parts of the group. One group that had this kind of process discovered they actually needed more structure and a decisive leader who could make linear decisions. The therapist/facilitator is able to bring out the identified roles of the group, represent the unwanted parts and allow the entire system to interact. This work often leads to greater community awareness and feeling.[1]

In a recent seminar a small group worked on their difficulties with one another. There was a lot of fighting. One woman sat quietly in the corner and looked on. In the overall atmosphere, this woman was the disavowed or secondary part of the group. When asked what she was feeling, she said that she was very sad and that it was difficult for her to sit in conflict situations. As she spoke, others who had been outspoken and angry began to nod their heads because they too had this feeling but were so attached to fighting that they had forgotten to notice their own unhappiness. When everyone had described their fear and sadness about conflict, the atmosphere transformed as the participants felt closer to one another.

Recycling values those aspects of our experience which we would normally take for granted. In a world where it is no longer harmless to throw away garbage, the therapist, too, recycles signals and information which are just outside

---

[1]See Arny Mindell, *The Leader as Martial Artist,* 1992, Chapter 5 for more detailed descriptions of group process and disavowed parts.

our ordinary awareness. Then she discovers the larger dreaming process that lies behind seemingly insignificant experiences.

Chapter Seven

PLAYFULNESS AND DETACHMENT

The spontaneity and freedom of the child are often put aside as we become adults and are frequently left out of therapeutic practice. This chapter begins with an example where the playfulness of the child emerges in both the client and the therapist. Afterwards, we will explore this metaskill and also the metaskill of detachment in greater detail.

THE EVIL WITCH

A European-American woman said that she felt quite distraught. She reported that she had just discovered a very wicked part of herself, a mean and evil witch. She had always known this witch was inside her, lurking somewhere in the background, and she had hoped it would never come out. She was afraid of it and hated it. What could she do?

Undaunted, Arny came up to her and, like an excited and curious child, said, "Wow, let's see that witch!"

"What??" she replied, "I want to get rid of it!"

"Yes, I understand," he said, "but just show me for a moment what that witch is like. You needn't stay with it long."

"OK, I warned you," she said. "You better watch out ... here it comes!"

The woman's face began to scrunch up, her eyes became beady, and her hair seemed to suddenly stand on end! As her face contorted, so did her body: shoulders raised, body bending over to the side, fingers curled in like claws! She shot a quick, menacing glance at Arny.

"Well, good morning!" Arny said with wide open, welcoming eyes. "I didn't know you were there! (Excitedly) Let's see what's in there!"

Arny then pulled slightly on one of the woman's gnarled hands to check what would happen. Suddenly the woman/witch grabbed him around the waist with all her might, and unexpectedly, lunging toward his knees, grabbed Arny around his legs. Arny caught his balance and a wild wrestling match ensued.

All the while, Arny followed the woman's energetic motions as she pushed him and they rolled together. The woman/witch inadvertently let out a few yelps and screeches and finally ... giggles!! Something was changing!

The woman no longer wrestled. Her forceful movements transformed into little jumps up and down. She laughed and screeched as she used the counterweight of Arny's arms to propel herself into the air and spring to the other side. They played and jumped together.

The woman glanced suddenly at Arny with amazement and he asked, "What is that glow in your eyes? Something's changed!"

She exclaimed, "I'm not an evil witch after all!"

"Well, what are you then?"

"I'm just a wild kid. I love to play and have fun and have someone to really wrestle and engage with! Gee, I cut that off when I was a child. I had so much energy and wildness but I stopped it because I thought girls weren't supposed to be like that. I long for that part of

me so much. It's so great to do it with you, to meet
someone who will play with me!"

"Yes," Arny said. "What looked like an evil witch
when we started was the beginning of a wild and playful
child who was trying to come out of you. She's beautiful! I love playing with her! What a joy to meet that
side of you!"

✳✳✳✳✳

There are many metaskills we could explore in this
example. You may have noticed the metaskill of compassion as Arny welcomed the part of this woman which was
disavowed—that is, the experience which she initially
called the "witch." Arny is not constrained by this state-
oriented description of her experience (see Chapter Six). In
fact, the woman's depiction of her experience as an "evil
witch" most likely originates from social categorization and
repression of women's energy and power. Therefore,
instead of remaining with this static description, they
recycle this information and through its unfolding discover
the joy and ecstasy of a playful child.

Arny is also in a playful and spontaneous mood. Now
let's explore the metaskills of playfulness, humor and
detachment.

Play

Playfulness and childlikeness arise in those moments when
we are inquisitive and excited about life. They reflect a
sense of freedom and spontaneity towards life's unexpected
events. In these moments we delight in the possibility of
discovering something new.

Psychotherapy is generally a serious business, with good
reason. We are all dealing with difficult and painful
problems, disturbing relationships, death, physical pain,
social issues and addictions. It seems blasphemous to be
happy or humorous in such situations. Yet, there is room

for the playful child who enjoys life, who relishes the moments of insanity, unpredictability, who has an outside viewpoint, who is detached enough to play for a while rather than get caught up in the everyday pain of life's events. Of course, bringing in a sense of playfulness demands that the therapist remain awake, notice the feedback from the client and adjust to this feedback.

The child frees us to go deeper into experiences that seem unchangeable. This experience of playfulness arises out of a particular world view which many of us had when we were children—an amazement and joy in the magical and unpredictable elements of life. Lao Tse reminds us that we must "become as a little child once more."

> The sage is shy and humble—to the world he
>   seems confusing.
> Men look to him and listen.
> He behaves like a little child.[1]

How exciting to grasp life as it reveals itself to us! How thrilling to discover the underlying process that is waiting to be discovered in this woman! Buddhists might call this metaskill "rapture" or:

> … zestful joy. A joyous interest in what's happening…
> The appreciation of the law, of the Tao, brings a great
> joy to the mind and cultivates the factor of rapture.
> Intense delight in exploring the truth creates a very light
> and buoyant state of mind.[2]

Playfulness and Freedom

Playfulness ushers us toward a sense of freedom from our ordinary identities and societal rules. The therapist's

---

[1]Feng & English, op. cit., Chapter 49.

[2]J. Goldstein, *The Experience of Insight: A Simple and Direct Guide to Buddhist Meditation*, Boulder: Shambhala, 1976, pp. 145-146. Thanks to Carl Mindell for pointing out this parallel.

attitude of playfulness might bring a change of working styles, open her up to irrational impulses and signals, allow something absurd to enter into the situation, or cause her to move, play or sing or simply feel more free as she is working. This could be a welcome relief particularly when she is feeling tired, stuck, or lost. Allowing this sense of playfulness to arise could open the way for new insights and information to emerge.

I remember a woman I worked with who was shy and said that she felt quite depressed. No matter what I suggested, she seemed to sink deeper into her depression. Feeling a bit stuck and tired, I began to follow my own impulses and to my surprise felt like a child who wanted to play. I asked the woman if I could explore my feelings a bit further. With her permission, I began to jump around and play with the toys in my consultation room. Suddenly the woman began to laugh and crawled over to me. We played and giggled together like little kids for quite a long time. The woman told me that she had become so adult-like and responsible that she had lost access to her child-like nature. As a result, she had become very depressed and uninterested in her life. She realized that she needed access to this playfulness to renew and instruct herself further about where her life was going and how to go about her worldly tasks.

Humor and the Fool

The metaskill of playfulness brings with it a sense of humor! Life can be fun, even funny at times. There have always been jesters, tricksters, clowns, comedians and mad people who are able to laugh and give us another perspective on our ordinary lives. Taoist writing is full of humor. The painter in China is "expected to be foolish, crazy, cranky or eccentric."[1]

---

[1]Rowley, op. cit., p. 14.

In the lovely book *The Way of Zen*, Alan Watts describes Zen paintings which capture this nonsensical, abandoned spirit. He describes the work of two artists who painted the Patriarchs and Masters of Zen as:

> ... abandoned lunatics, scowling, shouting, loafing around, or roaring with laughter at drifting leaves. As favorite themes, they adopted as Zen figures the two crazy hermits Han-shan and Shih-te, and the enormously rotund folk-god Pu-tai, to complete a marvelous assortment of happy tramps and rogues to exemplify the splendid nonsense and emptiness of the Zen life. [1]

Watts tells us that the constant theme of all Zen art is "... the aimless life ... expressing the artist's own inner state of going nowhere in a timeless moment."[2] In a sense, the Taoist therapist can also be a bit of a fool. She does not know where to go; she enjoys aimless wandering until life presents its chosen path. She is empty-headed and follows nature.

A number of modern day therapists such as Fritz Perls and Milton Erickson have dared to step out of the solely grave nature of the therapeutic encounter and show that life and therapy don't have to be drudging, painful and sober experiences. A therapist who is only serious may have a world view that life is always a solemn business. The therapist who notices his or her playful nature in various moments shows that life may also be joyous and thrilling. This therapist is sometimes happy and at ease—a mindless sage living from moment to moment with nowhere to go and nothing to do. Yet, this sage is fluid, a fool who manifests playfulness when it genuinely arises and switches to a sense of respect and earnestness when these arise instead.

---

[1] Watts, 1957, pp. 180-181.
[2] Ibid.

Every Day is a Fine Day

One of the most beautiful displays of this childlike, playful spirit that I have found was during a meeting that Arny and I had with a Zen Buddhist Master in Japan. When the Zen Master came in to greet us, his entire body was laughing; his mouth grinned, his eyes smiled and his whole being was enveloped in one huge belly laugh. What a joy to actually find the archetypal buoyant Zen master!

Where did this happiness come from? What was the belief behind his metaskill? When we asked him, he said, "Every Day is a Fine Day!"

This Zen master greeted every experience as if it were the right one for him to be having. He would say something quite serious and moments later burst into laughter. The belief that "every day is a fine day" reminds us to trust that even the absurd, the difficult, the painful and mysterious are meaningful if we are able to ride the waves of our experiences. If we are sick, if the weather is rainy, it may still be a fine day if we are able to climb inside these perceptions and creatively help them unfold.[1]

The Child at the Edge

The attitude of the child is a useful metaskill when assisting someone who is perched at an edge. That is, the person is about to experience a new part of her- or himself but hesitates and begins to fall back on her or his known identity. At the moment when new experiences arise and are blocked, it can be helpful to ask ourselves or our clients to pretend that we are children once again and could go over the edge into new experiences as a child would. This attitude reminds us of a time when many of us were free to experiment with life; events were not yet solidified, life

---

[1]Discussion with Keido Fukushima, Head Abbott, Rinzai Sect, Tofukukji Monastery, Kyoto, Japan.

was rich with surprises and fantasies. Playfulness could give us access to aspects of ourselves from which we are otherwise cut off.

Detachment

The child's mind and humorous attitude are related to another metaskill: detachment. Detachment is a particular feeling in which we are released from the apparent situation, when we step back and discover a "meta"—or outside—point of view. All of us notice a sense of detachment in ourselves in subtle moments when we sit back, feel a bit numb or trancey or have the need for an overview. Following this sense of detachment provides a perspective not wholly immersed in the ongoing drama of life.

Likewise, the therapist who only gets caught up in the suffering or primary process of the client may be less helpful than one who notices detachment in herself and stands back for a moment. A wider overview may provide information about aspects of the process of which she is not immediately aware. Perhaps she has become so embroiled in one aspect of what is happening that she has forgotten about other parts. Momentarily following her detached attitude, the therapist simultaneously steps out of her predictable ways of working and relating, becomes fluid once again and discovers an experimental, free spirit inside of herself.

Detachment is often associated with humor. The Yaqui Indian shaman Don Juan constantly laughs at his apprentice Carlos' seriousness and feeling of self-importance. When Carlos gets really serious or upset, Don Juan roars with laughter. His laughter comes from this sense of detachment. Don Juan tells Carlos, "As long as you feel that you are the most important thing in the world, you cannot really appreciate the world around you. You see like a horse with blinders, all you see is yourself apart from everything else."[1]

Humor and detachment bring a slightly *irreverent* but compassionate touch to our ordinary worlds. We not only stand respectfully by the primary process, which by itself would mean taking only one side, but we also stand firmly for the secondary process and its message. In the example above, Arny does not remain with this woman's fear of her "witch-like" side but helps her to unfold this experience to discover something new about herself. Humor and detachment are a way of telling our primary process that there are many worlds awaiting our discovery.

This outside, detached perspective is what makes comedians so funny. Have you ever noticed that, at the most serious and difficult times, a comedian will turn to the audience and say something so obvious that everyone roars with laughter? The comic removes him- or herself from the situation for an instant and says something inappropriate or irreverent—something which many of us are thinking but would never say because we are so entwined in our current drama.

Arny is one of the funniest people I know. Once he was working with a man who suffered from asthma. As the man began to describe what the asthma was like he demonstrated by pressing intensely on Arny's chest. When Arny encouraged him to continue, the man unexpectedly and excitedly said, "Are you scared I might do more?" Arny said slowly, "Well, the thought did cross my mind!" Everyone burst out laughing. Other times, I've seen Arny put his nose right in the middle of a couple who are poised, yet stuck in a long romantic look or a nasty fight and say in a quizzical, funny tone, "How's everybody doing in there? Is everyone in a trance? Anybody home?"

---

[1] Carlos Castenada, *Journey to Ixtlan*, London: Penguin, 1974, pp. 39-40.

Detachment and the Wise Older Person

I recently heard a beautiful story about the metaskill of detachment.[1] An aikido master from the United States went to Japan to refresh his skills. He got onto one of the subways in Japan and suddenly a big brute came hobbling down the aisle, drunk and threatening everyone. The aikido master was thrilled that he could finally put his skills into action, since he had never had the opportunity outside of his traditional practice.

As the brute and the aikido master were about to fight, a small, elderly man sitting on the bench looked up and asked the drunken man if he would come over and talk. The drunk threatened the old man, but was nevertheless intrigued. The elderly man asked him what it was that he had been drinking. The drunk replied, "Sake!" The old man smiled with delight, saying that he, too, loved to drink sake outdoors with his wife in the evening. The old man asked the drunk if he had a wife, and the drunken man said that he was alone and very sad. When the aikido master from the U.S. was about to leave the subway, he turned around and saw the drunken man lying with his head on the old man's lap, talking quietly as the old man stroked his head.

What had this elderly man done? He was detached from the potential danger of the situation. He did not take the aggressiveness of the drunken man at face value, but was detached from it, entered the man's world and saw that the drunken man needed a friend to comfort and talk with him. The old man recognized the drunken man's plea for friendship and help. The aikido master comments at the end of the story that he felt he himself was brutal and gross and would have to practice aikido from now on with a very different spirit. I would say that his metaskills were

---

[1]T. Dobson, "A Kind Work Turneth Away Wrath," *Lomi School Bulletin*, Summer, 1980, 23-24.

changing, from the attitude of fighting to win towards detachment and compassion.

Indeed, the metaskill of detachment is often associated with wisdom and age. We sometimes project this metaskill onto those who have lived a long time, who have seen many worlds and who have gone through so much in their lives that they have gained a sense of greater wisdom and freedom from the "doings" of everyday life. Yet, the metaskill of detachment appears in all of us at varying moments.

Detachment in Tough Spots

Detachment is an important skill when working with difficult situations. A detached sage or therapist is able to get into a hot pot and remain cool. This sage is able to be in tough situations with clients, in rough group conflict scenes or organizational difficulties and still access an outside viewpoint which can process what is happening.[1]

The metaskills of playfulness and detachment put us in touch with aspects of ourselves we might normally forget. They remind us of our childlike free spirits and also our ancient wisdom, which steps out and sees events from ever larger perspectives.

---

[1]Amy Mindell, *The Leader as Martial Artist*, 1992, and *Sitting in the Fire: The Politics of Awareness*, to be published.

Chapter Eight

FISHING

One of the central metaskills of the Taoist-type therapist is her ability to follow the quality of her attention from moment to moment as she is working. She will notice moments of intense concentration and other moments when her focus becomes diffuse and wandering. One of my colleagues, Nisha Zenoff, beautifully described the metaskill which follows the flow between these two types of attention as "fishing."

Have you ever gone fishing? You go out on your boat or sit on the dock, throw out your line and then just lie back and enjoy the scenery. Now is the time to relax and wait. Any good fisherwoman or fisherman knows that it doesn't help at all to get nervous and wait expectantly. You simply relax and let your mind drift off into the blue sky and deep waters. Occasionally the line moves a bit. You slowly get up and test the pole, to see if there is something tugging. If nothing is there, you return to a state of peacefulness and ease, waiting patiently once more. But the dynamic moment comes when a fish is really nibbling. This is the moment of action. You grab the line and focus on your task. With skill, deep concentration and great precision, you hold on and reel the fish in. The fisherperson is skilled only when able to both relax *and* concentrate.

The Taoist is an eternal fisherperson. She observes the changes in nature but does not act until the moment to act arrives. She is a minimalist who uses only the energy necessary to catch the fish. She can be both precise and easygoing. In the following example, see if you can follow the various moods of fishing. This case also provides material for our study of the metaskills in Chapters Eight and Nine.

HIDING UNDER THE MAT

Sue, a 22-year-old European woman, is slumped down in her seat. She says almost inaudibly that she wants to work on something, but does not move from her chair. Arny sits quietly as well. He looks peaceful, as if he has nothing to do. Sue continues to sit for a long time without talking or moving. She makes an inaudible comment. Arny looks around, seems a bit confused and continues to wait patiently.

After some time, Arny walks slowly over to her, tugs lightly on her pants and says, "Let's do something." Sue lethargically gets up and joins him in the middle of the circle. She says that she has been in pain in the afternoon because of migraines. She looks down, feels miserable, says nothing for quite a while and does not move anymore.

Arny pauses as well and waits. He starts to pace randomly inside the circle. As he passes Sue, he puts out his hand and says, "Let's go for a walk." Sue takes his hand and they begin to walk around the room. Sue's head is down and she walks very slowly.

Then something absurd happens. Arny notices a large mat lying on the floor. He bends down, picks it up and unexpectedly hangs it comically over his head. Sue immediately goes and gets another mat and does the same thing. Everyone in the room laughs. Arny then takes his mat and puts it over Sue's head, crossing the mat that is already on her head in the opposite direction. She immediately clutches both mats, holding them tightly to her head. We cannot see her face anymore, only her eyes peek out every so often. She seems to be using the mats to hide.

Arny notices how quickly she grabbed the mats and now with great interest and intent he comments, "Yes, do that and while you are underneath the mats, imagine what it brings you to have the mats over your head."

Sue studies her situation for a moment and replies, "If I stay like this, I can't be hurt."

Arny follows her fantasy and asks what could hurt her and she says, "My mother." Arny's attention has noticeably changed. He is now intensely focused on the story that is beginning to unravel.

"What does she look like?" Arny asks.

Sue drops the mats from her head and wraps one of them around her stomach and pronounces, "She is sort of fat!"

Arny comments, "That's nice you are showing me how fat she is, that mother." He picks up the other mat and holds it up partly in front of his face as if he were the child now protecting himself from the mother. A role switch has happened. Arny is now playing Sue and Sue is playing her mother. As the child, Arny says to the "mother," "Mommy, be nice to me."

Sue walks around the room as the mother, slowly and calculatingly. She exclaims, "NO!! I don't hear you, you are disturbing me all the time! I have to work."

Arny pouts as the child and replies dejectedly, "You're a fat old cow! Momma, you walk so slowly ... be nice to me, I need something to protect me against you. Why don't you like me, Momma? I'm just a girl."

Sue replies, "Get away from me."

Arny's level of upset mounts and he begins to scream and cry like a child, exaggerating both the humor and the seriousness simultaneously as he screeches behind his mat. "Ohhhh ... ohhh. AhhhhHHHH!!! MOMMA!!!!"

Sue walks up to him threateningly, pushes him away and says, "Go, GO!! I DON'T WANT YOU!!!" Arny shrieks even louder, exaggerating the fright. She continues to push him sternly away and then backs up.

Arny notices all of the energy in Sue's pushing motions. He knows that these motions may not have completed themselves. Now as the therapist he encourages Sue to really shove him. She is shy but starts to push him as he braces himself with his feet apart and his head down. He concentrates on her movements and on his inner-body sensations as she pushes against him. She says very definitively, "I WANT YOU OUT OF MY LIFE. GO!!"

Arny looks at her and says to Sue herself, "Wow, I heard that. That's a clear message. I knew you had the capacity in you to say that to people—to push things out like your mother! Want to try it again?" She hesitates, slumps down and holds her head. Arny, making a role switch, turns to the group and says as the mother, "It's great to have a daughter like that, she doesn't kick back too much when you kick her. She just develops terrible migraines." Sue drops down on the floor, holding her head in her hands. She seems to be at an edge. She is shy to use her force.

As Sue returns to her depressed state, Arny asks her if she can follow herself and report on what she is experiencing in her body. She says that her head hurts, that the pain in her head is like something holding in while something else is pushing out. She makes illustrative motions with her hands to describe this sensation of pressure.

Sue gets up and shows the motion of one hand pressing strongly against the other. Her face mirrors the tension in her hands. "Fascinating," Arny says. He mirrors her movements and facial expression and says, "This is what you look like. You look pretty strong." Sue grins. "You smiled," Arny says. "Would you like to have some of your strength? It might help your headache. Why don't you try it? Would you like to use it on me as your mother?" Sue says that she has to be nice to her mother. "Oh, yeah, I forgot about that. Well, just show that strength to me somehow."

Sue falls toward him and pushes. "Great," Arny says. "Now, can you stand and have the posture of somebody with force?" Sue begins to stand upright and clenches her fists. Arny encourages her, "Now, perhaps you could walk like that and make a face that goes along with it." Sue walks slowly, kicking her feet in front of her, looking sternly at everyone. Arny walks with her. She turns, walks straight up to him, looks intensely at him and then smiles.

"Great!" he said. "You can smile and do it at the same time. Now, how about taking this energy and moving with it ... letting it go ... pretend you could use it for anything. It doesn't just have to be against your mother." He makes strong motions with his arms, as if he is beginning a dance so that Sue feels accompanied in her movement. Sue's arms circle gently.

Noticing that she dropped the intensity of the movement and may have come to an edge, Arny says, "Looks very good, but perhaps you want to do it even stronger." Sue moves her arms strongly in front of herself, suddenly bending over and swooping around in circles, breathing out strongly each time she bends down, and then spinning around. Arny joins her and tells her to be creative and allow a dance or anything else to unfold.

Sue is intently involved in her movement as a very beautiful dance emerges. Sue looks something like a powerful blowing and somersaulting wind, jumping high and bending down low. Arny reacts to her wind power by falling over as she motions towards him. She loves the feeling of strength and the force of nature. She continues her dance, arms slicing the air like a samurai as the momentum spins her around. She begins to make punching motions in the air and then spins ecstatically. She is using all of her strength for a passionate dance. She glows with excitement, giggles and says, "I really feel better! This is what I need, to dance and express this energy creatively in my life! Thanks!"

$$*****$$

You may have noticed in this example the metaskills of humor and playfulness that were described in the last chapter. There are also other metaskills which will be discussed in the next two chapters. Let's concentrate now on the metaskill of fishing. Fishing is a fluctuation between two different kinds of focus. It is a combination of a diffuse, unhurried attention and a precise awareness. Let's explore each of these aspects in detail.

DIFFUSE, UNHURRIED ATTENTION

Arny is a relaxed fisherman in the beginning of the work with Sue. He waits. He looks as if he has nothing to do and nowhere to go. He follows his focus, which is diffuse and rambling, almost empty. Sue does not offer much information as she sits and slumps in her chair. He, too, sits calmly, as if he has nothing in his head, no goal or objective. He has no need to push or probe. He assumes that Sue will show him the way when she is ready. He simply waits for the "fish" to show itself.

This aspect of fishing is described beautifully in the *Tao Te Ching*.

Who can wait quietly while the mud settles?
Who can remain still until the moment of action?[1]

This unhurried quality is a defining characteristic of the sage. "Appearing stupid, he goes about like one who has lost his way."[2] Of course, the sage is not stupid at all. She or he knows that nature will show itself when it is ready.

---

[1]Feng & English, op. cit., Chapter 15.
[2]In Alan Watts, *Psychotherapy East and West*, New York: Vintage, 1975, p. 76.

This aspect of fishing reflects the background Taoist and process belief that we needn't work hard; the pattern or dreaming process is already there. We simply have to wait for it to appear in its own way.

In the *Tao Te Ching* we also read that the "Tao abides in non-action."[1]

> Thus the sage knows without traveling.
> He sees without looking.
> He works without doing.[2]

The fisherperson/therapist gets out of the way so the Tao can express itself. The fish will not be able to swim by if the therapist does not leave a space for it to swim in.

But what is the "fish"? The fish is the unexpected, spontaneous and numinous element of life that suddenly reveals itself. It is the secondary process, the first inkling of a greater dreaming process waiting to unfold.

The ability of the therapist to model this diffuse focus can be very important. Many of us are looking desperately for someone who feels it is all right to relax once in a while. The over-excited therapist gives us the impression that life is about hard work and a huge expenditure of energy. This is the metaskill of hurrying! Yet, it is quite rare to find a modern-day sage who can, even for a little while, follow the path of doing nothing and having nowhere to go!

Being Empty-Headed

This diffuse and relaxed attention could be described as empty-headedness. Noticing the moment when you feel empty-headed can be very helpful. Our desire to understand and be knowledgeable can, at times, be a block to following what is in front of us. We have so many ideas that we miss

---

[1]Feng & English, op. cit., Chapter 37.
[2]Op. cit., Chapter 47.

the process that is trying to unfold. When some beginning therapists in training seminars complained that they felt too stupid to know what to do with their clients, Arny replied, "Why should you know what to do? You shouldn't know what to do! Follow this feeling!" He said that the best therapists know the least. If you are too intelligent, you are not helpful. If you are too smart, you try to make something happen instead of following nature. You have an inflation that you are the creator of life instead of its assistant.

Process beliefs tell us that the process contains its own intelligence. We do not have to make something happen. On the contrary, we must discover the patterns of nature that are already there and make them useful to the client.

When we have this open and relaxed attention, we can ask even the most mundane sorts of questions, be lazy, unknowing, or naively fascinated by something new or absurd that catches our attention. This relaxed focus may show us a way it would be impossible to see if we were cramped and trying very hard to do something. It may help us notice signals that we would normally take for granted. In some of my training classes, I have encouraged students, after many intense weeks of study, to follow the sense of empty-headedness and to see how that attitude affects their work. Many reported a great sense of relief as they dropped their intentions and looked at the "fish" swimming by.

There is another advantage to being an unknowing therapist: it provides a great opportunity for the client to experience his or her innate wisdom. When the therapist does not know what to do, a great opportunity arises. Clients who normally depend on the therapist to create change and have an overview can learn about themselves and their own capacity for awareness. [1]

In any case, none of us feels intelligent all the time! The qualities of patience, laziness and "not knowing" are all

---

[1]From one of Arny's lectures on the failure of the therapist.

parts of our human experience. The challenge is to notice when they arise and to use them consciously in our work.

TESTING THE LINE:
MINIMALISM AND THE EFFORTLESS PATH

As the fisherperson's attention is relaxed, she or he occasionally tests the line to see if a fish is biting. Every so often in our example, Arny tugs on the line to test if the process will engage, if there is a fish on the other end, or if more time is needed for the process to unfold. If he tests the line and there is no response, Arny continues to wait. He approaches Sue and asks her to work on what is disturbing her. She gets up, but alas, remains sullen and depressed. The fish has not yet nibbled. He waits, then walks around, picks up a mat and suddenly the process has caught on.

This is a minimalist attitude which makes slight interventions, notices feedback, and lets go if there is no response. At this stage of the work, the therapist follows her instinct not to push forward. She takes the path of least resistance, requiring the least force and effort. Lao Tse reminds us of this metaskill:

> In the universe great acts are made up of small
>   deeds.
> The sage does not attempt anything very big.
> And thus achieves greatness.[1]

The therapist's work can be effortless. When psychology becomes too much work, it's no longer fun or engaging for you or for the client. Zen writers describe this effortless path as the act of folding neatly along the dragon lines or creases of the heavens, the natural path requiring no resistance.[2]

---

[1]Feng & English, op. cit., Chapter 63.
[2]M. Abe, ed., *A Zen Life: D. T. Suzuki Remembered*, New York: Weatherhill, 1986, p. 68.

Simplicity of style is crucial in Eastern painting. A minimal number of strokes evoke the essence of the painted subject in the viewer's mind. The least amount of effort is used.

> A simple fishing boat in the midst of the rippling waters is enough to awaken in the mind of the beholder a sense of the vastness of the sea and at the same time, of peace and contentment.[1]

When she is in this mood the process worker is like a minimalist painter. She does only what is necessary to test the water and follow the fish. She does not push the river, but tries to discover the natural path which suggests itself spontaneously in the work.

I remember a man who complained that he felt weak and lethargic. As we were working together, he said he didn't know what to do. I said, "Let's wait and see." At that point, he put his hands on his hips. The fish jumped! "That's it," I said. "What is it like to have your hands on your hips?" He said that he felt proud. I encouraged him to walk around with this proud attitude. As he did this, he suddenly became a heroic figure who could take on immense tasks. And so the work continued, as we unfolded the story of this heroic figure and what he could do in the world. I did as little as possible, got out of the way and allowed nature to express itself through this man's spontaneous movements.

Conservation of Information

The process worker is free to follow her emptiness and laziness because if she misses the fish once, there is no need to worry. The theory of conservation of information[2] tells us that information cannot be lost or destroyed but

---

[1]T. Mikami, *Sumi Painting: Study of Japanese Brush Painting*, Tokyo: Shufunotomo, 1965, p. 22-23.
[2]Amy Mindell, *River's Way*, pp. 84-85.

simply goes unconscious and will reveal itself soon in another form. Therefore, we can relax, knowing that information will appear again if we are awake enough to notice it. In Sue's work, the force that she manifested while pushing seems lost temporarily when she slumps to the floor in pain. It reappears, however, in her headache, which she describes as pressure.

Feedback

The central guidepost for any intervention is the feedback you receive. If you suggest something that is not right in the moment for the client, he/she will let you know through verbal or nonverbal negative feedback. You can continue anyway, but you will find yourself working harder than you would like, and perhaps never getting to where the client wants to go. The client may follow you, but is not totally involved in what is happening. Waiting for positive feedback may mean that you use less energy and follow the path of least resistance.

Blank Access

Noticing yourself going blank and sitting quietly for a moment can be very useful! This pause allows the client the space to express him/herself: a space in which to project and dream. Indeed, one of the essential qualities of the ancient master was being "hollow, like caves."[1] The spaces or voids in Japanese and Chinese painting are as important, or more important, than the lines themselves![2] Al Huang tells of the idea of "Brush Absent, Idea Present."

> This is a good time to think of the distinction between a solid line and suggested line. Which is more real? When I make a broken stroke, as in painting bamboo, the

---

[1]Feng & English, op. cit., Chapter 15.
[2]G. Rowley, op.cit., p. 72.

empty spaces between become very suggestive of something solid, like the joints of the bamboo. We describe this technique as "brush absent, idea present." We allow the white parts of the paper to suggest sky, snow, water or mist by painting dark areas of earth, mountain and trees. [1]

Similarly, Takahiko Mikami discusses the Japanese painting style, *Sumi*. He describes a picture of a sparrow as follows:

By giving him as much negative space as possible, you are permitting the little bird's freedom of movement— his existence. By painting one of these birds in one corner of a large area, you are giving him the space to fly up or down into.[2]

Empty space allows the viewer to delve into deeper realms of experience than can be expressed with paint and lines. The Chinese painting term *Hsu um* means "the brush comes to an end but the idea is without limit ..."[3]

The concept of empty space is discovered in a process work technique called "blank accessing." The therapist's momentary silence or minimal suggestion provides a blank space that the client can fill out with his or her own process and dreams.

When Arny asks Sue to take a walk with him, he is providing a blank access in movement. By asking her simply to walk, he allows her process to use the movement and the space to express itself in whatever way it would like. When he picks up a mat, Sue continues on this path and picks up another one. The story begins to fill itself out.

A blank access may be done in any channel and is especially useful in a channel that is unoccupied, or not

---

[1] Al Chung-liang Huang, *Embrace Tiger, Return to Mountain: The Essence of Tai Chi*, Moab, UT: Real People Press, 1973, p. 133.
[2] Mikami, op. cit., pp. 18-19.
[3] Rowley, op. cit., p. 77.

used by our ordinary awareness. In this case, Arny uses movement. It is in our unoccupied channels that the process appears most rapidly and spontaneously.[1]

CATCHING THE FISH: PRECISION

The third aspect of "fishing" has to do with a special focus that combines precision, clarity, and intent. When the fish is tugging on the line, when the moment to act comes, we must not hesitate.

When the time is right, the warrior shifts her attention, takes a stand and jumps. She notices the intense moment when the fish bites. She catches this dynamic moment with her awareness. She must act swiftly and hold on with concentration until the fish reveals its full nature. This precise attention requires the fluidity (see Chapter Eleven) to change focus rapidly and focus on the dreaming process that is trying to unfold.

Arny has said that if you are "only intense and focused, you will not attract the fish you want to catch." But, he continues, "If you are too relaxed, you will not notice that fish when it nibbles on your line!"[2] In fact, it is not possible to truly relax unless you are sure that you have the proper skills and feelings that will allow you to reel in the fish when it tugs on the line. The martial artist cannot afford to relax unless he or she is capable of acting instantaneously when the time to focus emerges. The interplay of these forms of attention is crucial.

What was the fish in Sue's work? The fish was the moment when Sue spontaneously put the mat on her head. Arny tested it by putting his own mat on top of hers. She grabbed onto them both. This was positive feedback. Something had bitten the line, the energetic process was

---

[1] See Arny Mindell, *River's Way*, pp. 22-24, p. 27, and pp. 133-134 for further discussion of unoccupied channels.
[2] Mindell & Mindell, *Riding the Horse Backwards*, p. 76.

beginning to unfold. Arny explored the process further by asking her what it was that she was doing. A whole story emerged and a big fish was caught!

Arny's earlier relaxed attention changed. He became centered on this dynamic moment and focused intently upon unfolding its contents. The empty, relaxed and minimalist mind allowed nature to reveal itself, and then switched modes and held tightly to its flow.

There may be many fish on the same line. Later in the work, when Sue is playing her mother and Arny is screaming like a little child, Sue quickly pushes Arny. Arny notices a new fish, another spontaneous happening! He holds on tightly and helps Sue identify with this pushing motion. He drops both the child and mother roles and encourages Sue to push even more and experiment with this energy. Courage is required to shift from one dynamic aspect of the process to the next emerging spontaneous signal.

The Second Attention

Arny uses Don Juan's language to describe the moment of catching and harnessing the energy of spontaneous events, for focusing intently upon numinous and unknown material. The therapist is a "tight warrior" who uses his or her *second attention*.[1] The first attention notices the primary "doings" of our world. The second attention grasps fleeting secondary material, holds on with intensity and allows these experiences to express themselves fully. It is a metaskill that says, "Yes, I know you are there and I respect you, I want to embrace your nature and help you unfold."

In relationships, the second attention might notice the forbidden or unexpected signals between the couple. In groups, the second attention could focus on the dynamic

---

[1]See Arny's *The Shaman's Body,* p. 39.

and perhaps fiery sudden conflict between individuals or a fleeting moment of silence that is disavowed.

The Path of Crumbs

A tight warrior uses his or her second attention to remain close to the secondary material that has emerged. Arny and I call this ability to hold tightly to the fish's trail *"following the path of crumbs."*

Do you remember the story of Hansel and Gretel? When Hansel and Gretel were being taken away by the nasty witch, the children left a path of crumbs through the forest so they would be able to find their way out once again. In process work, this means discovering the spontaneous process and focusing intently on its winding path.

Sue's case begins with the story of hiding and needing protection from her mother. Arny perceives this, and his job is to be a tight warrior and stay close to this story and the powerful energy that emerges from it. Arny notices that Sue spontaneously becomes the mother, and he finds out why the mother is so hateful. Then he does not stay with the mother's role, but remains with the central energy emerging from Sue. When Sue develops a symptom that turns into her own strength, Arny asks her if she can use that force against the mother. She says no. Staying close to this energy but following her feedback, he asks her to simply express her intensity in movement. By staying close to the energetic stream of her process, he helps it come to its own natural conclusion.

I remember a particularly vivid example from a recent supervision and training seminar for therapists. In this example, you will see Arny following the path of crumbs by noticing and staying close to the spontaneous, secondary experiences of this man—holding closely to the process as the man discovers new aspects of himself.

As Arny describes the idea of the path of crumbs, Tom, who is sitting across the room from Arny, asks a question.

Arny decides to use his question as a chance for demonstration. See if you can follow this path.

>Tom: (turns rapidly around to face Arny directly and says) I need just a little bit of help, Arny. I'd like to talk about my progress as a therapist.
>
>A: Sure.
>
>T: All right.
>
>A: What would you like me to talk about?
>
>T: Something about my development.
>
>A: (turns to the group and explains) This is a case in which the problem wasn't stated but was apparent. Did you see it? Tom turned quickly toward me so I'm going to guess, although I may be too fast with this and we will have to ask him, that one of the things that he's working on is turning directly and being direct in his life. (Tom nods immediately. Now to Tom, Arny says:) Does this match anything you know about yourself?
>
>T: Yes.
>
>A: It's possible, huh? Now do you know anybody that is really direct? Who can be as direct as possible and doesn't spend much time doing it?
>
>T: (Wonders) Hmm (and suddenly getting it) Yes, Arnold Schwarzenegger! (Everyone breaks out laughing.)
>
>A: Right! Now, I'm going to bet that Arnold Schwarzenegger is someone that may be interesting for you to get closer to. But before we do that, Tom, is there anything that has been keeping you from being Arnold Schwarzenegger? Who would be against that in you?

T: (Laughing) This is great! Um, let's see ... parents, father, mother, yeah.

A: I see. (Tom looks as if he is considering things) You're thinking about that. (Explaining his method to the group) I'm sitting now, not recommending one way or another, but going back and forth. I'm following him as the crumbs roll, and I'm sitting with him at this position.

Could you follow the dialogue so far? The initial crumb which Arny notices is Tom's quick, direct turn toward him. This is the incongruent, unexpected secondary signal that we do not yet understand, that leaps out and then hides again. Arny uses his precise awareness to grab this fish and stay close to its trail. He holds firmly to this moment and asks Tom if he ever knew someone who could be so direct. He is asking for a pattern, a model for this new behavior. Tom says that Schwarzenegger could do it. Arny asks about Tom's edges or barriers to this new experience. Who are the figures who stand at the edge and do not allow Tom to discover more about this part of himself? It is his parents. Having outlined the process of what is happening, Arny now sits patiently and watches to see how Tom's process will develop by itself. How will this "direct" quality unfold? The dialogue continues:

T: I noticed I just looked at you and you're another Arnold. Maybe you can help me with something.

A: I might be able to. How?

T: You are very direct.

A: So, I'm a person that can be direct sometimes. That's possible. (pause, Tom continues to look at Arny) I like how you're looking at me. Are you looking at me because you are seeing me? (Now to the group) I'm following the path of crumbs of his seeing, trying to follow his signals around this spot. (Again to Tom) Are you looking at me because you think I could help you with the next step, or are you in a trance?

T: I'm looking at you because I feel you are the way for me right now.

A: Yes, and what is it that you see about me when you look? Do you see my face, how I'm sitting, the color of my shoes, my bald spot? What do you focus on?

T: Your bald spot, I think!

A: Seriously? And what about my bald spot?

T: Well, I feel shy right now. I want to go on but I just wanted to stop for a moment because I feel I am putting myself out a lot.

A: I think you are putting yourself out an amazing amount. It's incredible you have gone this far and that you're aware of that. Do you think we should go back to where we were, or should we go back to the group? (Now explaining to the group) I'm going back and forth. You see, the psyche itself is very wise. It goes over an edge, has something like a trance, and then goes back to the primary process. This is the natural path. At a certain point it is too difficult. I'm going to make some recommendations about going over the edge and the job is just to sit with him at this point and notice what he does.

T: The bald spot represents to me the willingness to put yourself really out there. The head is exposed. That's really direct and going for it.

A: Yeah, that's me. (Humorously) I just go and do it. I've always had a tendency to do that. My bald spot ... I'm very vain you know! I ask

Amy about once a week how my bald spot is doing! I went bald in my early 20's. (To the group) Now it's relationship work. He's looking partially at me and partially projecting onto me and so now I'm coming in as myself, as a real person.

T: I have a bald spot that's growing, too. (He shows it to Amy)

A: It's a magnificent one!

T: I'm sort of vain, too.

A: So you have something like I do!

T: Yeah.

A: (To the group) He has a bald spot like I do, so we're getting closer to home. The next step would be to go home with that. (Amy means that soon Tom may be able to identify with this direct part of himself. Turning again to Tom.) Let me look at it.

T: The bald spot has been coming on for a while.

A: It's the growing part of you, the part that is exposed. And now I would ask you, at what stage are you in exposing yourself, how courageous do you feel, how far would be right for you to go? (To group) You see how this is a way of taking back a projection? (Again to Tom) How courageous could you be with clients? How much of that would be correct for you?

T: That's just what I feel my work has been about. I feel ... yeah ... (sits up straight looking sure of himself now, his voice raised slightly) like exposing myself now. I feel like I showed a lot of that when I worked in front of the group this morning as a therapist. I was very courageous. It's an edge to say that!

> A: I like the way you sat up when you told me about that. I am imagining that that signal is some sort of pride about yourself. Is that true? Do you feel proud of yourself? (Tom nods and sits up proudly) I like that you sit up with pride. I think it is very courageous to work in front of your colleagues at all.
>
> T: Yeah, I really feel that. Thanks, Arny.

We could not predict how Tom's process would evolve. Tom turns and looks at Arny and projects a directive figure onto him. Arny stays close to this new information by bringing himself in personally and allowing Tom to use his imagination as he looks at Arny. Arny follows the path but does not push. He wants to find out how Tom will deal with his edge about being more proud and courageous. Now that he knows what Tom is working on, what the fish is, he follows the method and the timing Tom has for discovering new parts of himself. The process weaves from Arny to the growing bald spot and finally to sitting up straight and feeling proud, direct and courageous. By following each crumb, Arny allows Tom's process to unfold in its own natural way and timing.

As a tight warrior, we can hold on precisely to the dynamic process that presents itself. Then we carefully and exactly help it unfold. It is clear from this example that the therapist who is able to stay close to the process and follow the path of crumbs can work rapidly, yet the wisdom of each individual's process determines how quickly and in what fashion the process of nature will unfold.

Going Fishing

The metaskill of fishing is a combination of different types of focus that occur naturally inside ourselves. When the empty mind arises, it signals relaxation and makes space for life to present itself. The relaxed therapist is a minimalist who lightly tests the water and waits for the fish. When the fish bites, she uses her second attention to hold the fish and help it unfold by following its unique, winding process. She follows the path of crumbs.

Chapter Nine

SHAMANISM-SCIENCE

Depending upon training and personal style, a therapist may tend toward a cognitive and analytical mode of working or toward a feeling and intuitive method. The former may be understood as a more intellectual or scientific way of understanding events. The latter relies more on inner feeling and spontaneous images or insights. Yet, the tendency toward one of these modes of working does not preclude the use of the other.

We notice the mind of the scientist arising when we try to understand material intellectually and put seemingly disparate elements together in a coherent fashion. At other moments we notice the tendency to drop out of what is happening and follow our inner feelings and fantasies, as we attempt to gain knowledge and understanding. This latter approach reminds us of shamans,[1] who leave consensus reality, go into trances and discover new infor-

---

[1]A shaman is a tribal healer who is able to fall into altered states, go into the underworld or world of the spirits, discover what is ailing the client, and then bring that information back to this world so that it will be useful to the client and/or community. Eliade, 1982.

mation for an ailing individual and/or tribe. Therefore I call
these two attitudes *the scientist* and *the shaman.*

This chapter suggests that these different attitudes arise
in most of us spontaneously. By consciously noticing when
each of these orientations is present, we can shift from one
to the next. A fluid therapist notices when she is
formulating ideas as to what is happening and will do this
consciously. She will also notice when her perception
changes, when she is unable to concentrate, when things
begin to happen in her which become so strong that she has
no choice but to follow them into unknown territory,
believing that they will guide her to greater awareness.
When patterns begin to emerge once again she may find
herself returning to her scientific mind, ordering and
understanding experiences analytically.

Consciously following these different attitudes creates
the metaskills of the scientist and the shaman. Let's return
to the example of Sue in Chapter Eight to discover these
two approaches.

THE SHAMAN

Toward the beginning of the work with Sue, she did not
provide much information about herself. Arny walked
around, suddenly picked up a mat, and put it over his head.
In this moment, he was allowing the shamanic aspect of
himself to arise, letting himself be moved and swayed by
the overall situation, trusting and following his seemingly
irrational impulses.

In this shamanic moment, the therapist dives into the
unknown and into mysterious territory. She does not know
what will happen but allows the moment, the overall
situation and her impulses to guide her. In process oriented
terms, she allows herself to be *dreamed up.*[1] She lets go

---

[1]"Dreaming up" refers to the experience when the therapist begins to
act as if he or she were a part of the client's process that the client has

and becomes a magical part of the overall atmosphere, allowing the situation to use her as a channel for its expression. Don Juan would say that she is entering the "*nagual,*" or the mysterious unknown, secondary world, as opposed to the "tonal," or the known, primary reality. She becomes something like a medium or mystic.

As Arny followed his impulses, he suddenly put a mat over his head. He did not think of this ahead of time but was moved in the moment to do so. He trusted that his impulse was not wholly irrational but a meaningful aspect of the *field*[1] trying to express itself. Indeed, we see that Sue picked up on the play with the mat, and from this seemingly "nonsensical" beginning, the process began to unfold.

By following the strongest signal in the moment the therapist may find herself focusing alternately on the client and then suddenly on herself.

> The discovery that what happens to you is part of me translates for the facilitator into the practice of being a whole person, being inside and outside the client's process at the same time ... movement, contact and

---

disavowed. The therapist can become dreamed up by incomplete signals of the client and react to them without even noticing the signals consciously. For example, the client may identify with leaning back and relaxing but be talking very quickly. Suddenly you as therapist find yourself feeling antsy, agitated and wanting to move. You may be "dreamed up" by the client to pick up information that he/she is not aware of, that is, the fast speed of his/her voice. See Arny's *River's Way*, pp. 41-44, for more on this.

[1] Arny describes the *field* as "an area in space within which lines of force are in operation. It is simultaneously everywhere with everyone. It is here and now in its entirety whenever we merely think of it. The world is you and me. It appears in dreams and body problems, in relationships, groups and the environment. And it appears through the feelings it creates in us when we are near sacred and awful places on earth. " *Leader as Martial Artist*, p. 8. See also pp. 15-20.

relationship are as important as inner feelings and dreams, and we place as much emphasis on awareness as on behavior.[1]

Indeed, process work theory tells us that the awareness of what is happening is more important than rules about what we should do. Debate about the validity of the therapist's inner states is replaced by the awareness of and meaningful use of these states for the overall therapeutic situation. In essence, there is no difference between what is outside and what is inside; we are simply becoming aware of and experiencing a field or dreaming process expressing itself through us.[2]

The key is to follow experiences we are having even if we do not understand their meaning ahead of time. Of course, if we would be impinging on the client, we must ask for permission first. The therapist uses her experiences in the service of the client.

The therapist as shaman allows the magical or mysterious to arise. She notices her inclination to trance out or focus on strange impulses and feelings and follows these to conclusion in a useful way.

Freedom

It is a great relief to follow our wandering awareness. We are free to drop what we are doing if it is not working and be more creative, to allow the unknown to arise. We are free to become spontaneous and imaginative people who follow the often mysterious path of nature.

Don Juan, a shamanic and unpredictable character himself, says that the person of knowledge is not tied down to known reality but is free to follow the spontaneous and unknown elements of life. Arny describes this condition as follows: "He is not at all like the animals he is after, fixed

---

[1]Mindell & Mindell, *Riding the Horse Backwards*, p. 22.
[2]Op. cit., pp. 22-25.

by heavy routines and predictable quirks, he is free, fluid, unpredictable."[1]

Non-linear Paths

This shamanic, unpredictable manner enables us to track the unique windings of any given process. More often than not, processes flow down non-linear pathways. As much as we try to be linear, clear, and analytical, the process often fools us and takes an irrational and unexpected turn. Without the shaman's awareness, we are unable to follow the unique course of the river. If we are grounded in shamanic awareness, we become part of the river and flow with it. Lacking such awareness, interventions may be geared more toward our ideas *about* process than to the momentary flow of nature.

If we are too fixed on understanding the process, we may not leave room for mysterious or unusual signals to arise. A therapist who employs only a scientific attitude may block aspects of experience that don't fit into known formulas and ideas.

I remember, for example, sitting with a client of mine. She was telling me about her daily life, which she felt was a bit boring. She spoke quietly and without much affect. For some reason, I could not follow her intellectually. I noticed my attention drifting. I asked her if I could follow my unusual sensations for a moment. She agreed. I had been paying close attention to her with my eyes and at this moment my head dropped, my eyes closed and I suddenly had a very strange image! I saw a picture of a large, nasty monster looming just behind this woman's head. The monster seemed to be threatening her. When I told my client this rather absurd vision, she said, "Oh, that is what I

---

[1]From an early manuscript of Arny's, *Deathwalk*, 1975, now published as *The Shaman's Body*, 1993.

dreamed last night! There was a big monster after me!" We then focused on this monster and what it wanted from her.

If I had tried to think analytically, I might have looked back and noticed how this "monster" already had appeared in this woman's behavior. Perhaps there was something in her words or her tone of voice or her movements which indicated this monstrous figure. Yet, I was unable to do this. Something drew me temporarily away from our conversation. By going inside myself, I discovered the monster that was chasing this woman. It turned out that this monster figure wanted to chase the woman out of her ordinary life and get her to be more creative in the world.

The greatest teacher of shamanism is nature itself. It propels us into absurd, unknown or magical pathways. Paradoxically, it is when we finally give up and learn to ride the waves of this unpredictable flow that the patterns and logic of the field begin to unfold. Who would have known ahead of time, in Sue's example, that picking up the mat would be the key to unraveling her story?

At another point in Sue's work, Arny encourages Sue (now playing her mother) to push against him. Although he has tried a number of times, she finally flops onto the floor, develops a headache and discovers this pushing energy once more. The concept of conservation of information (as mentioned in Chapter Eight) provides the freedom to let go, to allow nature to discover its own course, to step back from our linear procedures and let the mystery of nature find the path of least resistance, since the information will repeat itself in some other way.

A process guideline is: if you try an intervention three times and get negative feedback, the process is traveling in another direction; give up you are doing, drop your ideas, and follow the river's non-linear flow. In fact, this method happens naturally. If you encourage a client in a particular direction a few times, yet meet resistance each time, you will notice yourself getting tired and wanting to sit back. As you move back for a moment, you make space for the river to find its own pathway.

Inner Awareness

The shamanic-type therapist follows internal sensations, feelings and images and allows them to become guides.

While in physical contact with Sue, Arny's eyes are down. He follows his internal body feelings as his guide. He knows from the inside how much to push back, when to let up, and when to use a lot of force. There are many technical aspects of physical contact we must learn, but there is also an element of feeling that helps us know from the inside what is needed. Our internal body awareness is like a process gauge. When Sue begins to push Arny, he feels internally that she has not quite completed her motions. Therefore, he encourages her to push him even more until the pushing message is revealed. Of course, training in body and movement awareness is always helpful.

It is unusual for many people who have grown up in Western cultures to have this kind of internal focus either in their private lives or as therapists. Many people are trained *not* to focus on themselves when they are working with, or relating with someone else. Moreover, in Western cultures many people are trained more visually and less proprioceptively.

As the therapist drops out of consensus reality, she allows herself to follow the often spontaneous, unpredictable and non-linear path of any given process. She focuses on her inner-body sensations, movements and fantasies as guides and watches what happens with her client.

Let us now turn to the scientist, the counterpart of the shaman.

THE SCIENTIST

As we have seen, dropping out and following the dreaming process allows nature to reveal itself. Let's consider how the metaskill of the scientist complements and enhances a shamanic attitude.

Outer Awareness

In the moment that the therapist notices her scientific mind returning, even for a split second, she consciously allows it to emerge. Her scientific mind is exact. It is able to discern what is happening while a process is unfolding. She can look outwards and grasp patterns that are appearing, notice feedback from the client, see edges that can be explored and help the overall process to deepen.

The scientific viewpoint tries to discover structure and content. The therapist in the scientific modality should consciously support and follow it in detail. The exacting nature of the scientific mindset can achieve a special kind of clarity.

Retaining Your Periscope

Arny sometimes refers to scientific awareness maintained within the context of the shamanic attitude as "retaining your periscope." You go down under the water, let the waves move you, but maintain a periscope that can catch the minute feedback, reactions and signals of the client. Don Juan's term for this is "controlled abandon"—letting go while still having some element of alertness.

With Sue, Arny allows himself to follow his spontaneous impulses and put the mat over his head. Sue does this, too. Arny does not get lost in his mysterious play, however. His scientific mind awakens when Sue puts a mat over her head. At this moment he enters—and follows—the dreaming process with a scientist's clarity. He is aware of the structure of what is happening: someone is hiding and therefore someone must be threatening. Two parts of Sue are in conflict with one another.

Going to the Depths

Without access to scientific clarity, we could cycle in shamanic feeling or imagery states which are important, yet may not be sufficient to go to the depths of our processes. We could play around with Sue, alternatively putting mats and chairs on our heads, but might not pick up the central issues that are trying to unravel. We could remain with Sue's experience of being a sad child (her primary process) and not discover the power and creativity (secondary process) that she has inside herself. Or we could stay with her painful migraine headache without discovering the energetic dance inside this pain.

Role-playing, too, relies on the complementary modalities to be effective. As shaman, the therapist enters the feelings and thoughts of the role. If she has access to the scientist, she will notice how the client reacts to this figure. I call this "dual awareness." The therapist is in a role while talking *about* the role—metacommunicating—at the same time. At one point in our case example, Arny plays the child and Sue plays her mother. Arny acts like a child while simultaneously commenting on the slowness of the mother's walk and her forceful push. He plays the child while concurrently keeping his awareness clear and *talking about* the mother's behavior.

Of course, leaving the scientific realm and going into a shamanic mode can be equally relieving and bring a depth to a process which was as yet unattainable.

Arny describes the shamanic and scientific attitudes in *River's Way*:

> Being a phenomenologist, a process scientist is a sort of mystic and an empirical, rigorous scientist in one. He determines the existence of channels whose exact nature may never be completely understood and thus works

with phenomena whose ultimate origins may even be unthinkable. He tries to follow the course of the river and adjust himself to its flow. He listens carefully to sentence structure, watches body signals, uses his hands to feel the dance of life and his imagination to explain his own responses.[1]

THE SHAMAN AND THE SCIENTIST

The shamanic and scientific paths are very closely connected. If a therapist begins with a scientific approach, she may give up and follow the spontaneous wanderings of the Tao when her mind can no longer follow what is happening in the moment. She begins to dream and follow her inner sensations, fantasies and movements, but does not get so lost that she is unable to notice feedback and make the information useful to her client.

Of course, it is impossible to prescribe the emergence of the scientific or shamanic mode. It is up to the therapist to notice when either the shaman or the scientist arises and to follow these with awareness. Some are more gifted in one than the other. The development of a fluid relationship between these two metaskills is a matter of time and experience.

---

[1]Amy Mindell, *River's Way*, p. 28.

Chapter Ten

CREATIVITY

This chapter discusses our everyday life experiences as the seeds of creative expression. The process worker attempts to discover the energy of our body problems, relationship issues, and dreams and find the creativity behind them. Therapy is not only a means to problem-solving or self-knowledge but provides access to our creative potential. By acknowledging and joining the energetic stream of our experiences, the therapist becomes a co-creator in life. She transforms the energy of processes into dance, art, music or other creative modalities. Life as a whole becomes a regenerative, creative process and therapy becomes a lively and artistic endeavor.

Do you remember the moment in Chapter Eight when Sue, near the end of her work, transforms the energy of her headache into movement? Arny encourages her to take the energy in her headache and pushing motions and use it creatively. She dances like a whirlwind as therapy transforms into art.

Likewise, Arny does not remain static in his therapeutic role but is free to be a creative and lively force in the process. He spontaneously joins and reacts to Sue's movements as they create a wind-dance together. This is the metaskill of creativity. While encouraging clients to become and experience as much of themselves as they can, the therapist is also free and models the ability to follow her creative impulses and lead an artistic life.

Creativity: When Psychology Becomes Art

The contributions of movement, art, music and expressive arts in the field of psychotherapy open us up to the importance of artistic expression in the helping professions. The focus on creativity suggests a new paradigm in therapy that redefines its boundaries.

In fact, Arny says that he is not doing psychology anymore; psychology is something he used to do. Now he is a process worker, following whatever is happening. He writes:

> ... since healing, therapy and medicine continue to play important if limited roles in our interactions with people, they must combine with art, music, clowning, politics, group and religious experience to be more useful and meaningful. Let's face it. Anything less than fun burns out and bores creative therapists, and drives them to give up a profession which could be really exciting![1]

The therapist can paint, sing or dance as she, too, follows the energetic stream of life inside of herself. If she encourages her clients to be as free and creative as possible, it would be incongruent for the therapist to remain static and unbending.

Free Mind, Creative Mind

Where does creativity within the client and the therapist come from? What belief lies in the background? In his

---

[1]In an early version of Mindell & Mindell, *Riding the Horse Backwards*.

interpretation of the term *"mushin,"* the Zen master Keido Fukushima called it "free mind" or "creative mind"[1] in contrast to the traditional translation "no mind." His concept of "free mind" is very close to the metaskill of creativity.

The free mind is one that is not attached to any particular identity but free and open enough to pick up and identify with the flow of the Tao. Our Zen Roshi told us, if you want to know who you are, when you look at a mountain, become a mountain. If you notice a rainy day, become a rainy day. On the back cover of a beautiful book entitled, *A Zen Life: D. T. Suzuki Remembered*, we read Suzuki's words:

> ... man thinks yet he does not think. He thinks like showers coming down from the sky, he thinks like the waves rolling on the ocean, he thinks like the stars illuminating the nightly heavens; he thinks like the green foliage shooting forth in the relaxing spring breeze. Indeed, he is the showers, the ocean, the stars, the foliage.[2]

The metaskill of the "creative mind" allows you to join what you are experiencing, become it and actually create with it. You are no longer a passive observer, but a living, creative force in nature itself. Sue experienced a whirling motion and as she followed this movement, she herself became the whirlwind. Her process left the bounds of her known experience and entered into expansive creative possibilities.

This is the artist: one who is able to discover the shifts in nature's energy, begin to ride them, and create with their energy. The artist is not a victim of her/his fate but becomes a co-creator of life. The free and creative mind is not attached to any identity, to primary or secondary

---

[1]Personal communication, Kyoto, Japan, November, 1990.
[2]In M. Abe, ed., op. cit.

material or solutions to problems, but rather fluidly joins the flow of the dreaming process.

Names, States, and Energy Work

Why not remain with the static figures and states of the mother, child and headache, which came up in Sue's work? Behind the intensity of the mother, the pain of the headache and the reactions of the child, we discover the same quality of energy in different forms. This forceful energy is the thing that initially troubles and disturbs Sue, and finally, it is this energy itself that she comes in contact with.

The tendency to label aspects of ourselves with static names (as mentioned in Chapter Six) can be an important stage when we need to understand and analyze parts of ourselves. Yet the dangers in labeling a particular form of energy—for example, a "nasty mother" or a "headache"— are that 1) certain internal experiences may be labeled and frozen into one narrow container which may or may not fit each situation, 2) it becomes difficult to get inside the container and help it evolve, and 3) it is difficult to let go of the name and use the energy behind it creatively—to be fluid in joining with our experiences. We are reminded of Lao Tse's warning about getting attached to the names of things instead of the essence behind them: "The Tao which can be named is not the eternal Tao."[1]

In fact, the names of processes may confuse us. We do not know, for example, if Sue needs to be more like her *mother*, to use the anger of the *child*, to investigate the relationship between these two parts, or to concentrate on her *migraine*. From a process standpoint, the same energetic force lies behind each of these states.

The concept of energy plays a large role in many body-work schools of modern and ancient times. These body-oriented directions focus on the energy streams and path-

---

[1]Feng & English, op. cit., Chapter 1.

ways in the body, seeking to remove blocks in order that energy can flow more fluidly.

A process worker in a creative modality discovers the energy already present in our blocks, disturbances, symptoms, secondary figures and signals, stays close to these energetic spots by working on our edges and then uses this energy creatively. Process work is not about going from one bank of the river to the other, i.e., from one figure to another. It is about getting into the river, following it and living in its dynamic flow.[1] As we come in contact with the fluid process behind our experiences, we discover the dreaming process, the energy and creativity behind dream images, symptoms and problems.

The Taoists were well aware of this essential energy behind all events. Indeed, they viewed the Tao itself as "a seamless web of unbroken movement and change, filled with undulations, waves, patterns of ripples and temporary 'standing waves' like a river."[2] Any momentary configuration of the river is impermanent.

> Like streaming clouds the objects and acts of our world are to the Taoist simply shapes and phases which last long enough in one general form for us to consider them as units. In a strong wind, clouds change their shapes fast, in the slowest of the winds of Tao the mountains and rocks of the earth change their shapes very slowly— but continuously and certainly.[3]

This flowing energy of the Tao is often depicted in artwork as streaks or dragon lines which flow through the object or painting. These streaks or lines symbolize the

---

[1] Amy Mindell, *River's Way*, p. 6.
[2] P. Rawson & L. Legeza, *Tao: The Chinese Philosophy of Time and Change*, London: Thames & Hudson, 1973, p. 10.
[3] Ibid.

stream of the Tao which is "not confined within individual things but permeating them all."[1]

Another useful analogy is found in modern physics. Physics describes the interplay between states and energy in the particle/wave phenomenon.[2] Depending upon how you look at an electron, it will appear as a particle or as a wave. A psychological correlate would be as follows: depending upon when and how you look at a particular aspect of a process, it will look like a particle, a dream figure or state, (in Sue's case the mother, the symptom or the child's anger) and at another time it will look like a wave, or some sort of energy trying to express itself (her dynamic energy which finally expresses itself in dance).

The therapist's job is to notice when the "particle" aspect and when the "wave" aspect of a process is arising. In Sue's work, the focus on the interaction with the mother or the headache did not go further. The most fluid route, finally, was creatively exploring the energy behind these events.

Sue is in the middle of understanding and confronting the various figures and issues in her story. This is one important part of her work. Yet another aspect of her experience is the connection with the life-force behind these events; the thrill of riding and flowing with the river of life. We need an awareness that can fluidly focus on the particle and the wave aspect of process.

The Symptom Creator

The ideas of energy and creativity are intimately linked with the study of acute and chronic symptoms. Research in process work has shown that every symptom has at least two parts. There is the victim—or the one suffering from the pain—and the symptom maker, who gives the pain. If

---

[1]Op. cit., p. 17.
[2]See F. Capra, *Tao of Physics*, Toronto: Bantam, 1984, pp. 55 & 136.

we momentarily get in touch with this symptom maker (instead of remaining in the victim standpoint), we suddenly discover an immense amount of energy that can be used.[1]

Do you remember the man in Chapter Five who worked on his symptom of shivering? When he got in contact with the symptom creator—the shaker—he no longer shook himself. Instead, as he identified with the one that made the shaking, he discovered an enormous untapped energy inside himself, which finally turned out to be a desire to become a politician.

Another man, about 60 years old, worked on chronic asthma, which had plagued him since he was a child. When he became the maker of the force that pushed him from the front and back of his chest, he experienced a tremendous exhilaration and a lot of energy. He continued with this "pressure" energy and suddenly jumped around and began to turn cartwheels! Who would have thought that so much creative, playful energy would be tied up in his asthma? What a shame not to connect with it!

Relationship Work

Working with the dreaming process in relationships can be surprising when it is allowed to express itself creatively. I remember two women who had just met each other. They introduced themselves and had a rather pleasant conversation. When they followed their secondary body signals, one of them became very shy and the other became very animated and direct. As they followed these signals, a really funny dance ensued. The shy woman scampered around and the animated woman jumped up and wanted to grab the shy woman. As the process unfolded, the roles switched. The shy woman became interested in playing and

---

[1]This idea of Arny's arose shortly after he wrote *Working with the Dreaming Body*. It has not yet been recorded elsewhere.

scampered after the earlier animated woman (who was now shy). The two went back and forth in a beautiful dance of getting to know one another in childlike play. It was lovely to see the dreaming dance behind their relationship!

Therapist as Artist

In various moments, the therapist discovers a "free mind," one that is able to ride the waves of the Tao, to jump in and be creative. In this moment she is like an artist who picks up on the energy of what is happening and then creates with the spark behind it. Like the Chinese painter, the therapist may go beyond the surface of events and discover the essence, the energy, behind the form.

> To become a bamboo and to forget that you are one with it while drawing it—this is the Zen of the bamboo, this is the moving with the "rhythmic movement of the spirit" which resides in the bamboo as well as in the artist himself.[1]

This painter does not identify with the bamboo itself, a static form, but is moved by and conveys the energy, rhythm or spirit inside it. The martial artist penetrates to the essence of each animal or universal pattern that he or she is mirroring rather than simply imitating it.[2] The Japanese haiku poet uses a few words and syllables to express a moment—an experience—that cannot be grasped in ordinary language.

The therapist who connects with her creativity does not just sit back and watch life go by, but grasps her own surge of creativity as it arises. She is not content with static descriptions of experience but gets in and flows with the

---

[1] D. T. Suzuki, *Zen and Japanese Culture,* Princeton University Press, 1973, p. 31.
[2] H. Reid & M. Croucher, *The Fighting Arts*, New York: Simon & Schuster, 1983, p. 90.

dreaming process behind them. She is an artist or poet, joining the energy of the river, free to jump in and explore, dance, sing and play. In so doing she discovers something new and unexpected.

Integration

Sue's example reveals a layer of process work that notices states and figures, yet ultimately connects to the flow of nature beneath all manifest events. It then goes one step further, not only noticing this energy but creating with it. We do not become passive boat riders on the river but actively create with the river's waves.

What does this mean in terms of integration? Traditionally, integration means discovering a new part of yourself and then using that part in your everyday life. Process work presents another view of integration: the integration of *awareness*.[1] This means that the parts we discover are important but finally integration signifies the cultivation of *awareness* of the ongoing stream of process throughout our lives. We can tap into and follow the energetic force that streams through us and through our relationships at any time, any moment.

In Sue's work, integration meant noticing when, for example, this wind-energy arose, grabbing hold of it and in that moment following its energy rather than making a prescriptive behavioral change. In terms of the therapist, this awareness means noticing her feelings change as she works and allowing these feelings to manifest and unfold in a useful way.

Integration, in this sense, is the ongoing awareness of the dreaming process as it arises throughout our lives, whether we are in therapy, at work, or at home. It is a focus on the dynamic and changing movement inside of us and our ability to transform it into a creative force in all that we do.

---

[1]See Arny's and my *Riding the Horse Backwards*.

Life becomes a continual, regenerative and creative endeavor. Arny says:

> If you do process work, you are interested in the total life process and this means you are not interested in just one train station. You want to go the whole line. Your process can bring you everything you need in time. If you learn to follow your process without aiming at one station, or goal, then you become an individuated person. Your life becomes richer...[1]

The therapist who notices the metaskill of creativity inside is as interested in behavioral change as in riding the dynamic energy of life. She is an artist who follows the images and states which arise and also the energy behind them. She offers the client the possibility of creating with this energy as she herself is also free to create, to dance, and follow the dreaming process. As she uses the metaskill of creativity, she becomes a model of living a creative and spontaneous life.

---

[1] Arny Mindell, *Working With the Dreaming Body*, p. 32.

Chapter Eleven

FLUIDITY AND STILLNESS

Process work is based on discovering and unfolding unique changes in nature over time. How do we adapt to this stream of change? How will we be flexible enough to follow the spontaneous and unexpected windings of our experiences. What metaskills do we need? In this chapter, I describe two metaskills which help with this task. The first I call "fluidity" and the second, "stillness."

Once again let's look at an example and then discuss these metaskills in greater depth. The following is a delightful illustration of group work with about fifteen four-year-old children. Notice how Arny discovers the spontaneous process of the children and helps it unravel in story form.

THE TEDDY BEAR AND THE WAY BIG BEAR

As Arny entered the room, the children were a bit shy. They weren't sure who this new adult was. Slowly, different children started to show Arny their teddy bears. He admired them. Then one girl threw her teddy bear in the air. Arny said, "How fascinating the way the teddy bear jumps in the air! That's new for me!"

149

Almost immediately, all the children gleefully threw their teddy bears in the air. Arny began to weave a story about a teddy bear that could fly. He used blank accesses (Chapter Eight) to allow the children to fill in the various parts of the story with their own fantasy.

> Arny: If you sit down, I'll tell you about one special teddy bear that could fly. (All the kids sit down. One child offers her teddy bear to Arny, which he uses to demonstrate the dramatic elements of the story). Once upon a time there was a very special teddy bear that could fly in the air like this. (He shows this with his bear) The teddy bear flew all around. And do you know where it went?
>
> A Child: To the zoo!!
>
> A: (Using the feedback from the children) Yes, he went to the zoo! The teddy bear looked all around and do you know where this teddy bear decided to go?
>
> Another Child: In a house!
>
> A: Yes, in a certain house in the zoo. So the teddy bear went in and looked around and do you know what the teddy bear saw?
>
> Another Child: A bear!
>
> A: Yes! A bear! How big was that bear?
>
> Same Child: Way big!!
>
> Another Child: Bigger than a cloud!
>
> A: A very big bear! The teddy bear saw this "way big bear." And what do you think the big bear did then?
>
> Child: He ate the little bear!
>
> Arny: Did he do it? Let's see if the big bear ate the little teddy bear or not. (Arny begins to move slowly and heavily like a big bear. Suddenly, one boy jumps up. He goes behind Arny and pushes him. Then the child begins to

wrestle Arny until Arny is flat on the ground. The other children roar and cheer. The child who has wrestled Arny to the ground victoriously holds him down with one hand and shows the muscles of his other mighty arm to the rest of the group.)

The Child: I got you!

Arny: (Still on the ground and unaware of what the child is doing, turns around and seeing the posture of the child says) Yeah! Now everybody can see the great hero fighting to save the teddy bear!

The story continues and other children wrestle Arny (as the big bear) to the ground as they feel their strength and discover their heroic powers again and again.

✳✳✳✳✳

As small children, many of us felt quite powerless in comparison to the adult world. As their story unfolded, the children switched from being "small bears" to identifying momentarily with the "way big" powerful energy that is inside themselves. They realized that they, too, are capable of being great heroines and heroes.

The reader will notice the metaskill of creativity discussed in the last chapter. Arny joined the creative and playful spirit of the children as he entered into the bear story. He helped develop the story, acted out different parts and expressively engaged in its unfolding as it turned and spun to conclusion. He used blank accesses such as: "The teddy bear flew all around. And do you know where it went?" to provide empty spaces the children could fill in with their own process. In this way, the bear story is continually created by the spontaneous movements and fantasies of the children.

Let us turn now to the metaskills that allow us to follow the flow of the children's process as it evolves over time.

FLUIDITY

Fluidity refers to the therapist's feeling ability to move, adapt and flow with the unique curves and windings of any given process. Quite often, a process begins in one spot and then streams onwards into many different pathways and expressions. Of course, the attitude of fluidity cannot be programmed but must be discovered as it arises naturally in the therapist.

A fluid therapist is spontaneous. She is not bound by set ideas and programs about what should happen but adjusts to whatever is happening in the moment. Arny noticed the children's shyness and also the way that the girl threw her teddy bear in the air. This was the unexpected signal with which the story could begin. By following the children's process, he discovered a story that was inherent in the children's group rather than creating his own story from the outside. Each step of the way, he provided space for the children to fill in their own feelings and imaginations, and he fluidly shifted and changed the story accordingly.

Taoism

A fluid therapist learns to be like a river, following the flow of signals and processes as they carve their unique path. We are reminded that, to be good Taoists, we must become fluid like the Tao and connect to this essence of change. As Wilhelm says, "It is in constant change and growth alone that life can be grasped at all."[1]

In their book, *Tao: The Chinese Philosophy of Time and Change*, Rawson and Legeza tell a wonderful story from the Taoist writer Chuang Tzu which illustrates the metaskill of fluidity.

---

[1]R. Wilhelm, ed. *I Ching or Book of Changes*, London: Routledge & Kegan Paul, 1973.

One day Confucius and his pupils were walking by a turbulent river which swept over rocks, rapids and waterfalls. They saw an old man swimming in the river, far upstream. He was playing in the raging water and went under. Confucius sent his pupils running downstream to try and save him. However, the old man beached safely on the bank, and stood up unharmed, the water streaming from his hair. The pupils brought him to Confucius, who asked him how on earth he had managed to survive in the torrent among the rocks. He answered, 'Oh, I know how to go in with a descending vortex, and come out with an ascending one.' He was, of course, a man of Tao.[1]

The authors continue to explain that "... the ideal Taoist is he who has learned to use all his senses and faculties to intuit the shapes of the currents in the Tao, so as to harmonize himself with them completely."[2] But how difficult this is! It would be so much easier to have a set plan and stick to it. Many of us understand life in terms of objects and states. And yet life itself always teaches us that nothing is permanent. The Taoist learns to understand and appreciate life as it is happening, as it is changing, transforming and moving.

The Taoists spoke of this metaskill in their description of a yielding quality which we can cultivate in life:

> A man is born gentle and weak.
> At his death he is hard and stiff.
> Green plants are tender and filled with sap.
> At their death they are withered and dry.
> Therefore the stiff and unbending is the disciple of death.
> The gentle and yielding is the disciple of life.[3]

---

[1]Rawson & Legeza, op. cit., p. 11.
[2]Ibid.
[3]Feng & English, Chapter 76.

Therefore, the fluid therapist yields and changes as the current finds its pathway. We are reminded of the difference between states and processes. States are static pictures of a greater dreaming process. It is the process worker's task to notice these state-oriented descriptions but to connect with the moving energy inside our experiences. Indeed, process work is based on the flow of perception.

The Flow as Teacher: Effortlessness

Fluidity in process work derives from the central belief that the process itself will point the way. We needn't push or have great ideas about what should happen. Rather, by following the signals and signs along the way, we find the path revealed to us. Our task is simply to adjust to it.

This sort of awareness should bring an effortlessness to our work. As Blofeld says:

> To go along with nature effortlessly, as does a fish or a master artisan, is to swim with the current, to let one's knife slip along with the grain. When nature is taken as a guide, a friend, living becomes almost effortless, tranquil, joyous even.[1]

Indeed, Arny has said that when we don't catch the waves of the process, we suffer as therapists. We feel that our work is off track, that we are pushing or working too hard. In this example, following the children's process is just like effortless play. He discovers their natural path and simply assists it as it unfolds. If we find the process inherent in any individual, couple or group there is no need to push or "make something happen." It happens by itself!

Using Channels and Channel Changes

The metaskill of fluidity requires not only flexibility and openness but also the skill to observe channel changes. The

---

[1]Blofeld, op. cit., p. 10.

fluid therapist follows the process as it winds its way through many different channels. It may express itself in a body symptom such as a migraine, in dialogue, in movement, in pictures, or sounds.

> If you do not know about channels, then you will work only physically, or only with the dreams of your client, and you'll miss the bends and turns in the river, which make all the difference in the world.[1]

For example, I remember a woman who worked on her experience of physical pain. When Arny asked her how her body felt in the moment, she looked up quickly. In this moment, she had a visual access to her body feelings. Therefore, they began by making drawings of her body experiences. While she was drawing, she made long sweeping motions and her process turned suddenly into movement work. Eventually her movement work led her toward interaction with other people, hence, relationship work.

If we follow these channel changes we discover various therapeutic forms. We suddenly find ourselves doing something like art therapy or dance therapy, Gestalt role play or music therapy. Many kinds of therapy emerge if one follows whatever presents itself.

> In a way, process oriented psychology is nothing unto itself, but produces whatever is happening in the moment: Buddhism, Jungian psychology, NLP, Gestalt, Rolfing, Hakomi or anything else we have not yet dreamed up. Psychological methods are patterns inherent in all of us at given times.[2]

Ultimately, process work is like a river that has no character of its own but takes its exact form from the signals and channels of the given moment.

---

[1]Amy Mindell, *Working with the Dreaming Body,* p. 11.
[2]Op. cit., p. 22.

On Not Being Stuck

From the process work point of view, it is not possible to be totally blocked in following a process. If you imagine water running down a path, it may become obstructed by rocks, but will always find its way along a new pathway. It may take a surprising route, but nevertheless it continues to flow. There are moments, of course, when we must sit with something for a while and not move. The *I Ching* calls this Standstill or Stagnation.[1] Yet, if you are *aware* of this dynamic moment, then you are not really stuck at all!

There are a number of reasons that you may feel blocked and not fluid in your work. Let's take a look at some of them.

You may be at an impasse because you are trying to work in the wrong channel as mentioned above. I remember a woman who had cancer. She said that she did not think cancer was a big problem. She would not work somatically with her body experiences. She would not work visually or in movement, but she did talk about her troubles at home with her children. Her process was flowing freely in the relationship channel.

Hence, to work with individuals it is useful to know something about different channels. If you work with movement, you may also need to know something about the relationship channel. If you are able to work with relationships, then you will also need to know how to work internally with a person who is not relating verbally. Working with individuals in comas requires a knowledge of inner work as well as body and relationship work.

Another reason for feeling stuck is that the process may be expressing itself through you and your feelings. You may, however, be so intent on the client that you do not fluidly shift your attention and notice your own feelings. I remember feeling blocked when a client told me many

---

[1] R. Wilhelm, op. cit., p. 52.

stories about her past. The work did not seem to be going anywhere. After listening for a long time, I noticed that I was feeling very tired and told her that. She said, "Oh, me, too, I am tired of all my stories. I just want to relax and enjoy myself." The river opened up and began to flow again.

Another reason for being blocked may be that the process is trying to change levels between individual, relationship and group work. For example, in working with an individual who continually complains about relationship issues, it might be important to bring in the person's partner and actually do relationship work instead of concentrating only on this individual's psychology. Large group work may get blocked because it is asking for a change toward individual or relationship work.[1]

The fluid therapist becomes a living example of following, changing and fluidly moving with the current of the Tao. She opens to the spontaneous signals of the Tao and flows like a river down a mountain. Without this fluidity, life becomes static and clutched. She is always working against the current, unable to follow herself or her clients. Yet to have the freedom of fluidity she also needs a sense of "stillness" in the midst of constant change.

STILLNESS

To be fluid, we also need to both let go and remain centered, to give up forms and concepts and ride the waves of nature while maintaining a steady awareness that remains quiet in the flow of events.

The fluid therapist has a still center that perceives the emergence of new information. She remains awake in the midst of change. In the case of the group of children, Arny weaves the story, yet notices each new input from the

---

[1] See Arny's *Leader as Martial Artist* for more information on the interplay between individual and group work.

children. When he wrestles with the first boy, he turns around and watches what the child is doing and continues to unfold the story with this knowledge. He is both flowing and still.

Meditation in Motion

In the martial arts we find the complementary moods of fluidity and stillness. The founder of aikido, Ueshiba says:

> In the fluid movements of aikido there is always a firm center. A sense of balance pervades every motion of the hand and foot and they glide smoothly, as if in a dance, because the movement of the whole body is nothing but the smooth movement of the center. I believe the main point in aikido is the realization of a strong, firm center.[1]

The combination of fluidity and stillness appears in many traditions. Once again we are reminded of Don Juan's attitude of "controlled abandon."[2] This is a special mood in which a warrior lets go of himself while retaining a quiet center.

Process work calls the awareness which constantly monitors the overall process the *metacommunicator,*[3] the part of ourselves that is able to talk about and comment on what is happening. The metacommunicator is a neutral part which remains outside while simultaneously being inside turbulent waves. We are immersed in the process while having an outside vantage point that can help processes unfold.

> ... if you can act deliberately in the midst of a secondary process, instead of floundering helplessly in its power,

---

[1]Ueshiba, op. cit., p. 35.
[2]Carlos Castenada, op. cit., pp. 134-135.
[3]Amy Mindell, *River's Way*, pp. 19, 84-85.

you are harnessing its strength while maintaining your identity.[1]

Lao Tse says "the ten thousand things rise and fall while the Self watches their return."[2] We also find this concept of a still center in the practice of "momentary concentration" in Vipassana meditation and also in the mindfulness of a Vipassana walking meditation.[3]

Remaining Alert in Altered States

Remaining alert in the midst of movement or chaos is particularly difficult when dealing with strong altered states of consciousness such as rage, depression, ecstasy or mania. We get swept away by the stream and are unable to find the way back to our neutral center. I remember a client I had who was very angry at her partner. She suddenly reached out and wanted to wrestle with me. I was not prepared but somehow joined her in her movement. As she grappled with me, I noticed that she was not only wrestling and pushing me but subtly pulling me to her. I commented on it and she put her attention on this unexpected change in our movement process. As she focused on the movements of pulling me closer, she began to cry. She said that she was not just angry but was actually a very warm person. She was shy to express her deep feelings of love and warmth toward her partner. Her mood visibly changed and we focused in greater depth on these feelings.

Maintaining awareness in movement is a most difficult task. Many therapists have little awareness in movement and are unable to maneuver and focus their attention in this altered state. If we are unable to notice secondary movement signals and edges, the process may cycle endlessly without going to the depths of the work. Training in

---

[1]Op. cit., p. 41.
[2]Feng & English, op. cit., chapter 16.
[3]Goldstein, op. cit., pp. 4-5.

movement for those people who are not accustomed to it is helpful.

The metaskills of fluidity and stillness in motion are crucial to all process oriented work. Whether focusing on a group conflict, a relationship difficulty, a chronic symptom, or working with ourselves alone,[1] we are challenged to flow with the changes in the river while retaining a still point around which processes can unfold.

---

[1] See Arny Mindell, *Working on Yourself Alone: Inner Dreambody Work*, London: Penguin(Arkana), 1990, for details about inner work.

Chapter Twelve

THE CASTLE OF HAPPINESS

As I come to the end of Section II, I notice my own spontaneous desire to throw in one more example that touched me deeply. To exemplify trusting my feelings in the moment, I will jump in, write the case, and hope that it will be of use to you.

Try a self-test. What metaskills do you find in the following example? Can you identify some of the metaskills we have previously mentioned: compassion, recycling, playfulness, detachment, fishing, shamanism, science, creativity, fluidity and stillness? Perhaps you will notice other metaskills that I have not mentioned. I will leave you with this example before turning to the task of learning metaskills.

> In a seminar on chronic symptoms, a 40-year-old woman named Ellie who had cerebral palsy wanted to find out more about the connection between her physical symptoms and her life myth. Cerebral palsy is a nonprogressive movement and postural disorder resulting from brain damage. Ellie said that cerebral palsy did not affect her ability to think.

To find out about a person's life myth, it is helpful to ask about early childhood memories or dreams.[1] Ellie remembered repeatedly dreaming as a child that she was in a castle with her whole family and having a really good time with them.

Arny asked her how she experienced her cerebral palsy. She said that cerebral palsy made it impossible for her to move easily and spontaneously like everyone else. She said that she has to think first before she is able to move. She must think of where she wants to go and only then can she begin to move her body. It is a constant strain and tension to always be alert and mindful of her goal and how she will get there. She said that this is her way of getting along and adapting to normal culture.

To follow her *actual* experience of cerebral palsy, Arny asked her what would happen if she would move without thinking first about her goal. Ellie wasn't sure. She said she would be interested in finding out what would happen if she did not have so much pressure to concentrate. She was afraid, though, that she might fall.

Arny asked her if she would feel safe enough experimenting with movement from a seated position on the floor so she could not get hurt. She agreed, sat down, and began to turn slightly and twist. As she moved, you could notice a special way that she used her fingers that did not seem quite congruent with the rest of her movement. Arny encouraged her to follow her fingers and as she focused on them they began to touch Arny's head and then to massage it!

---

[1] Arny has spoken about his research into the connection between the earliest childhood memory or the earliest remembered childhood dream and mythic patterns that the person experiences throughout her or his life. Though we have seen this connection in hundred of cases, this work has not yet appeared in Arny's writing. See Alan Strachan's article, "The Wisdom of the Dreaming Body: A Case Study of a Physical Symptom," pp. 53-59, *Journal of Process Oriented Psychology*, Fall/Winter, Vol. 5, No. 2, 1993.

Suddenly she said, "Oh, that is what I dreamed last night! I dreamed that I was touching your head!"[1] Suddenly Arny had the feeling that there were actually two people massaging his head! He followed this feeling and had a fantasy that the other spirit was an older sibling. Ellie replied that she was the oldest child but that her mother had had a miscarriage before she was born. Arny imagined that the spirit of this older sibling moved with Ellie. She felt soothed by this thought.

Arny encouraged Ellie to continue to move as if she were letting something else direct her. He encouraged her to notice anything unusual that came up and follow it. After a couple of minutes Ellie found herself moving sideways on the floor. Then she wanted to stand up. As she experimented with "letting herself be moved" while standing she continued to move sideways and exclaimed, "Gee, it is actually very easy to move like this!"

Ellie laughed and laughed. She didn't have to think but could simply move with ease. She said that she had been trained to go forward which always required a lot of attention, and it was amazing to allow her body to move as it wanted and travel sideways! She stressed over and over again that it felt "so good!"

Arny said, "Yes, that's the idea! Have the freedom to do whatever feels good, whatever it might be." Ellie said that if she would just follow what made her feel good she would start to dance, but she didn't want to dance alone. She wanted everyone in the group to dance, too. The group began to clap their hands and dance, and everyone sang a sort of rock and roll song. It was a

---

[1]Ellie told me later that she used to rub her father's head in the same way that she rubbed Arny's. She said that her father really loved her no matter how many times she fell down or how she talked. She said she felt she could just be herself and knew that her father loved her. She told me that she felt the same kind of love from Arny and that rubbing his head was her way of telling Arny how special he was to her.

joyous atmosphere. Ellie danced in the middle in the most passionate and ecstatic way!

Finally, Arny commented, "This is your childhood dream! You were with your family in a castle feeling good! Your body is trying to do things that feel good and bring others into that castle!" Ellie glowed with happiness.

✳✳✳✳✳

We have focused on specific metaskills found in Taoist and process oriented therapist's work. The next chapter asks, "Is it possible to learn metaskills?"

Section III

BECOMING A
SPIRITUAL TEACHER

Chapter Thirteen

LEARNING METASKILLS

When you use metaskills and bring your moment-by-moment feelings and attitudes into your life and your work, you are a spiritual teacher modeling the ability to live your deepest beliefs in all that you do.

Can a person learn to be a spiritual teacher? This depends upon learning to follow one's ongoing flow of feeling attitudes. While the metaskills mentioned in Section II may be desirable for a therapist and, indeed, for *all* of us in our personal lives, in actuality most of us are rarely detached or fluid except for brief moments. We may want to be Taoists, yet find ourselves holding on, attached and clinging to every situation, thought or identity that comes our way. Some people develop these metaskills in time, while a few have them from the beginning.

What, then, does the learning process entail? Let us first address the learning process of the therapist-in-training.

Beginner's Dilemma: A Mountain Is Not A Mountain

No matter how glorious the path of learning, training to be a therapist can be an arduous task, full of challenges, fears,

ups, downs, and some amazing moments of clarity. I am
reminded of an old Zen saying:

> A Chinese Zen master once said: "Before a man studies
> Zen, to him mountains are mountains, and rivers are
> rivers; after he gets an insight into the truth of Zen
> through the instructions of a good master, mountains to
> him are not mountains, and rivers are not rivers; but after
> this, when he really attains to the abode of rest,
> mountains are once more mountains, and rivers are
> rivers."[1]

I don't know how many times I have thought of this
saying throughout the past years. It speaks to my own
development as a therapist and the development of many
other therapists-in-training I have seen.

What does this curious Zen saying mean? Before I
started my training, life seemed very simple. People were
just people. They had problems or they didn't. A mountain
was still a mountain.

When I began my private practice years later, my view
of people had changed immensely. What used to look like
an ordinary person had became a conglomeration of parts
and processes which I could barely decipher. Life had
grown more and more complicated. My list of theories and
techniques continued to lengthen. There were attitudes I
hoped to attain and others that plagued my work. I felt that
I would never be able to master even one small portion of
the immense knowledge, skills, and feelings necessary to
deal with the vast range of human experience. I was
fascinated and distraught!

I noticed that *trying to work* with people inadvertently
became more important than the people themselves! Arny
remarks about the beginning therapist:

> The novice student of process work generally faces two
> basic problems. Firstly, he may feel responsible for

---

[1] T. Thien-an, *Zen Philosophy, Zen Practice,* 1975, p. 90.

something happening and feel he should play creator. Then he 'pushes,' that is, he tries to recommend new ideas and therapies so that processes will occur. Or, he becomes impatient when things finally do happen and does not give them a chance to perseverate. If he ignores perseverations he will not learn from events themselves what and how to amplify. In this case he compensates for insufficient observation and lack of patience by applying standard procedures which are not tailored to the individual situation. Then his work becomes erratic and exhausting. In either case the student therapist suffers from feeling too important.[1]

In other words, many student therapists seem unable to follow the attitudes that arise inside themselves, and instead apply techniques artificially to try to make things happen.

So here we are, in the middle stage where a mountain is looking more and more like a maze which we can hardly find our way through! What should we do now?

Wouldn't it be better not to begin training at all? After all, some beginners work beautifully just because they still have a beginner's mind. A mountain is a mountain to these people. Some people are so healing to be around that it may be a shame to train them, for fear of losing their gifts. They already have all the metaskills one needs to be a true healer.

Yet if we return to our original definition of psychotherapy as the combination of metaskills and techniques, we will need to go into training to foster both of these and help them grow. As in a spiritual discipline, we must learn the tools of our trade while simultaneously developing and transforming ourselves.

What should this training include? I do not know entirely. For safety's sake, let's look first at the attitudes that stop us from learning.

---

[1] Amy Mindell, *River's Way*, p. 96.

Hindrances

After observing myself and many therapists-in-training, I have noticed innumerable hindrances, the first of which is our attachment to succeeding. Even the best student with the best intentions, when faced with a real human being, struggles furiously, pushing and pulling until utterly exhausted.

Every spiritual discipline has obstacles to knowledge and enlightenment. Don Juan[1] identifies the hindrances as the fear of losing clarity, the fear of the unknown, the drive for power and the tiredness of old age. Goldstein[2] cites the hindrances to meditation as sense desire, hatred, sloth and torpor, laziness of mind, sluggishness, restlessness, worry, regret, agitation and doubt. The Taoist would probably say that ambition is the greatest hindrance. The Zen archery master might tell us that the beginning archer is not connected to the deeper principles behind her/his art and therefore cannot yet perform archery in the proper manner.

One of the most common hindrances for the therapist-in-training is mistaking the *techniques* of following the Tao for the Tao itself. She begins to think that channels, signals, edges and feedback are the true Tao instead of mere vehicles for uncovering and discovering the Tao's flow.

How can we learn if we are lazy, ambitious or impatient? Some say it is through rote learning, others discipline. Who really knows?

Using Our Blocks

The process paradigm would say that it is only *through* hindrances, that we learn to follow ourselves and the Tao. To be truly congruent you must notice what is happening inside yourself even if you think it is ridiculous and only

---

[1] In Arny's *The Shaman's Body,* pp. 91-108.
[2] Goldstein , op. cit., p. 51.

your process.[1] You must pick up your feelings and attitudes and use them as metaskills. You will be less useful as a therapist if you are not yourself with all your quirks and meanderings. So, in some ways, you have no choice.

How might this look? I remember a supervision seminar geared toward the learning process of therapists. In the seminar, therapists-in-training worked with clients in the middle of the room and then received feedback about their work. In one particular case, the client was seriously depressed. No matter what the therapist-in-training did, the client sank deeper and deeper into her depression. The therapist was extremely goodhearted and tried and tried to help her client, but under the weight of constant negative feedback sunk into her own depression.

Arny asked the therapist what it was that she was experiencing. She said, "I am so sad, I want to be helpful but I feel I can't do anything useful. I'm getting hopeless." Arny said, "Well, how about experimenting with following your process and really giving up! Follow your feeling attitude and bring it in consciously!" This is the core idea behind metaskills! The therapist complained that she didn't want to give up but realized that she couldn't do anything else.

She actually did give up consciously, slumped on the floor and said that there was nothing more she could do. At that moment, the client burst out laughing uproariously! "What are you laughing at?" the therapist asked.

The client replied, "As I look at you, I see myself there on the floor and you look ridiculous and I just want to have fun in life!"

This unexpected switch happened only when the therapist followed her process of feeling like a failure and collapsed on the floor. At that moment, the client was freed from her identification with her depression and was able to

---

[1]Mindell & Mindell, *Riding the Horse Backwards*, p. 230.

access this other, joyous side of herself. Then the therapist continued to slump on the floor as she simultaneously helped the client experience this lighthearted part of herself more fully.

If we notice attitudes inside ourselves which seem to hinder our work and use them with awareness, we become process workers. We have recycled our own feelings and learned to follow the Tao.

Becoming a Taoist

By noticing and utilizing the feeling attitudes inside you, you may discover in yourself some of the metaskills described in this book. The therapist in the example above learned something about letting go and hence the metaskill of detachment. She no longer tried so hard. By following her feelings and getting out of the way, she allowed the river to find its own path.

At some point, you might feel a bit dimwitted, not knowing what is happening with your client and not knowing what to do. By consciously using these feelings you discover the metaskill of the "empty mind"; perhaps this emptiness will make way for even greater perception. The empty mind or fishing metaskill lies *in potentia*, waiting to be picked up at moments of "not knowing." It may be your greatest guide!

If you allow even the most absurd behavior inside yourself to unfold, you may discover the shaman or the playful child. The intense desire to understand what is happening, if used consciously, may develop into the exacting scientist. Noticing these attitudes and using them as metaskills will give you greater access to all of your skills. It is when we exclude these attitudes that we tend to get blocked and cut off from our overall awareness.

The Metaskill of Learning: Compassion

But how can we notice and cherish our feeling attitudes? We need the metaskill of compassion! Without a compassionate attitude towards ourselves, we cannot embrace the troublesome states we get into as beginners. We are not open to the parts of ourselves that are strange, shamanic, weak or inexplicable. Can we compassionately embrace our hindrances and turn them to gold? Can we love the absurd inside ourselves that gets in our way?

But what a problem! It is most often the beginner who does not have compassion for her or his slow learning process. Perhaps a really good teacher will help you develop it. In the absence of this, here is another possibility.

Maybe the only alternative is to not accept ourselves, to push our feelings and attitudes further back, to ignore our impulses, to criticize ourselves and try to act like a computer program. When this effort exhausts us, we notice a compassionate attitude emerging spontaneously. To let the process teach us what to do when we are not able to follow the Tao, Arny suggests that we try to go *against* the flow. We should push and shove and try to change ourselves as well as our client. Only then, having fully exhausted ourselves, and having lived through many difficult situations, do some of us give up and ride the river.[1]

If you are utterly attached, then be attached. If you do it consciously, this is the metaskill of attachment! Hold on for dear life until you are exhausted. Then you will once again let go and join the streaming river as it flows on to another territory. Live your attachment. It is the key to your individuality and finally gives you access to all of yourself.

In one of our training seminars, a therapist noticed that he was attached to being really present and listening intently to his client. He exaggerated this feeling by leaning forward and listening closely. Then he found himself

---

[1]Op. cit., pp. 231-232.

becoming detached and even wanting to turn away. The client said that he would like the therapist to experiment with turning away. There was a long pause and suddenly the client said, "Goddamn it, pay attention to me! I'm important!" The client said that he had never been able to stand up for his own needs and feelings before. As the therapist followed his flow of feelings and brought them consciously into the work, the client was able to explore and express a new part of himself.

It's a challenge to use your feeling attitudes consciously. If you are criticizing yourself, why not step out and actually do it? Perhaps then you will be free of this incessant, irritating voice. You may discover that the critic is a part of the client's process too. If you find that you are unable to think clearly, why not nurture the shaman inside of you? If you are tired of therapy, maybe the artist is trying to peek its head out.

Individual Learning Paths

One of the central tenets of process work is that you cannot do it unless you are really yourself. Your own personality and individual working style are crucial to therapeutic work. Process work is not a set of tools or a behavioral prescription, but a path which should enhance the person that you are. The best therapists follow themselves, can be utterly mundane or very spiritual, and use their own process and personality in conjunction with their techniques as tools of their trade.

Each therapist-to-be has a unique path of learning. She or he will work fluidly and naturally in certain areas, will be gifted in particular metaskills and will have less access to others. Some learning paths are linear while others take very non-linear and unexpected turns. For instance, if you concentrate on a scientific attitude towards your work, you may suddenly become blocked in order to investigate a shamanic approach.

If you are interested in the metaskills in this book—in the deeper spiritual beliefs and Taoistic attitudes behind therapeutic work—you have these metaskills inside yourself. Yet exactly how the underlying beliefs of process work manifest depends a great deal on your own individual style. How compassion will reveal itself through you as a unique person may be very different from how it will appear in someone else. Each metaskill must turn upside down and backwards inside of you and come out with your individual touch.

Every therapist, painter, or musician will express her/his art in a very specific way depending upon her/his understanding and interpretation of the skills and metaskills. Process work should look different when different people practice it. Indeed, if everyone who is practicing process work begins to look alike, we know that something is wrong; people are not really following themselves or the basic feelings and beliefs behind their work. Yet all Taoist-type therapists are united through their belief in the spontaneous flow of nature.

Regardless of one's art, a fluid practitioner has melded the methods, tools, and beliefs of a given trade with his or her own unique personality. Therapists who are open to their changing nature and attitudes can flow and transform from moment to moment as they work.

Life and Experience

To really become a Taoist-like therapist, we may have to be patient and wait. The pathway towards integrating and living any discipline—martial arts, painting, dance, music, writing or psychotherapy—may take time, experience, and perhaps many other elements that cannot be predicted.

I don't think I have been much of a Taoist in my life, but after years of working with people and seeing many amazing things, I think I am slowly becoming one. Life itself may be the best teacher of metaskills.

Most learners can, or perhaps must, read about the Mystery schools of modern and ancient times, study Zen, Buddhism, Taoism, shamanism and the martial arts. But frankly, we think that the impossible challenges of life are the best teachers.[1]

I have noticed that difficult and painful group conflicts, relationship issues, working with the dying, chronic body symptoms and, most of all, living life with all of fate's surprises, quirks, joys and pains have been my best teachers. Life imparts the metaskills necessary for our work.

A Mountain is a Mountain ... Again: The Spiritual Teacher

After stumbling through our learning process—trying, experiencing, repeating and then allowing our learning to become saturated with our own personalities—we hope to find ourselves at the stage of "the mountain is a mountain" once more. What a relief! We aren't preoccupied with parts of people, techniques, metaskills and ideas: we simply live in the ongoing flow of life. Like any skilled therapist, musician, martial artist or poet, we no longer think of the isolated elements of our trade but live spontaneously in the sea of our beliefs and experiences.

There is a Japanese phrase I find wonderfully descriptive of this stage. It is *ma o shimeru*, "to eliminate the space in between." It means doing "the right things without any space between thought and action."[2] It depicts the moment when the moonlight hits the water, creating a reflection. There is no time between the appearance of the moon and its reflection in the water.

We act when the moment is right. We allow our beliefs to move us in particular ways. Our attitudes become meta-

---

[1]Ibid.
[2]Kushner, op. cit., p. 51.

skills, enriching our work. Our techniques and skills grow out of this earth, spontaneously from the moment. Our work constantly changes and transforms, depending upon each situation. Everything we do springs from our underlying beliefs. We are spiritual teachers who live our deepest beliefs from moment to moment, revealing the beauty in sometimes troubling and often awesome experiences.

The therapist-to-be is like the student of martial arts or meditation, Zen or Taoism—on a spiritual path. It is a path of learning, struggling and finally loosening ourselves from the grip of what we have learned in order to live fluidly in accordance with our basic beliefs. We use feelings and techniques to follow nature, ride its uncanny waves and discover the sacred in life's most ordinary events.

Chapter Fourteen

TEACHER, ARTIST & FOOL

The concept of metaskills is a new vehicle for expressing our deepest beliefs in therapy and in life. This concept arises out of the principle in process oriented psychology which says that the feelings which arise in ourselves are potentially meaningful if we allow them to unfold. Metaskills give an appreciation for the feeling life of the therapist. Through training and awareness, these feelings become integral to the fabric of a therapist's work. Feeling attitudes are not just passing moods—not at all! With the new concept of metaskills, they are elevated to the level of skills, they are the spiritual art of therapy. Metaskills make other techniques possible because they are their vehicle. Yet training is crucial to learn how to follow feelings and make them useful in helping others.

As mentioned previously, the practice of psychotherapy may be defined as the unique combination of skills and metaskills of a given therapist. Metaskills alone are not enough. Working with someone in an acute psychotic state certainly requires the therapist's feeling awareness, but also, especially, her skillful ability to use her techniques. Yet techniques alone leave therapy a lifeless, mechanical interaction without the spirit and beliefs that make it meaningful. The practice of therapy, then, is based both on a feeling wisdom *and* an intellectual wisdom.

Focusing on the interactions between feelings and techniques helps to clear up discrepancies between what people say they are doing and what they actually do in therapeutic practice. Perhaps strict classifications of therapeutic systems will break down as we discover more similarities and differences in the way we actually work with people.

The Therapist

If we focus on metaskills, in what way must our definition of the therapist change and expand?

When techniques and metaskills combine, therapeutic practice becomes exciting. It is full of energy and life as it transforms from moment to moment. This new therapist has no definitions about herself before beginning to work. She allows the process to teach her what is needed, which transforms therapy into a creative and exciting endeavor. At one moment she is a therapist who sits down and discusses analytically the various problems of her client; in another moment she may look more like a dance therapist or artist who steps outside the boundaries of problem-solving and joins the creative element of life. The practice of psychotherapy evolves into a spiritual discipline of following and using our feelings and techniques in the service of the client.

This therapist is neither serious nor insightful by definition. Rather, she uses her awareness to follow and apply her attitudes and techniques. She hopes that her clients will discover their whole selves and live creative regenerative lives, and she models the same freedom. Her inner experience tells her that life is as full of problems and answers as of passion, madness and creativity.

Spiritual Teacher

By believing in her experiences and bringing them usefully into her work, she is like "the moon in the water." In that moment of awareness, she is a direct reflection of her most heartfelt beliefs. Her spiritual ideals find footing in practical work.

Clients come to therapists seeking the answers to problems, looking for meaning in life, wanting to clear up relationship issues, or looking for ways to delve more deeply into the core of life. The client seeks a guide, fortuneteller, companion and therapist.

The role of the therapist expands as she becomes something like a spiritual teacher. She models the capacity to bring spiritual ideals into our everyday world. Like Buddha, she embraces all forms of life. Like a Zen master, she teaches about the simplicity and beauty of nature. Like a Native American healer, she stops the world and dives into the unknown. She is a quintessential Taoist master who respects and follows the flow of nature and who cries, laughs and embraces her own failures.

Artist and Fool

Metaskills enable fundamental Taoist and process oriented beliefs to find footing in practical work, creating a therapy which is at times shamanic and scientific, fluid and still. This therapist can be thrilled by the rapture of life, chuckle at the human condition and play in its waves. She is a Don Juan-like figure who surprises the world with controlled abandon. She is a madwoman who dives into the mysterious and uncanny parts of life with ecstatic revelry. We witness the unique wisdom of the joker and the fool, the wonder of the child, as well as the zany creativity of the artist.

Using metaskills, we discover that they apply not only to therapeutic work but to life as a whole. Metaskills

constitute a lifestyle. They are not reserved for psychotherapists. Any individual who believes in his or her feeling
states can bring them to life in daily interactions. Life
becomes a regenerative, creative act of discovering and
rediscovering ourselves and living our spiritual beliefs.

BIBLIOGRAPHY

Abe, M., ed. *A Zen Life: D.T. Suzuki Remembered.* New York: Weatherhill, 1986.

Ansbacher, H. & R. *The Individual Psychology of Alfred Adler.* New York: Basic Books, 1956.

Bloch, S. *What is Psychotherapy?* Oxford and New York: Oxford University Press, 1982.

Bodian, S. "Field of Dreams." In *Yoga Journal*, March/ April 1990, pp. 66-72.

Blofeld, J. *Taoism, the Quest for Immortality.* London: Allen & Unwin, 1979.

Blum, H. "Psychoanalysis." In Kutash and Wolf, (eds.), 1986, pp. 3-21.

Bugental, J. *The Art of the Psychotherapist.* New York: W.W. Norton, 1987.

Capra, F. *Tao of Physics.* Toronto: Bantam, 1984.

Carkhuff, R., & Berenson, B. *Beyond Counseling and Therapy.* Holt, Reinhard & Winston: New York, 1977.

Cartwright, R. & Lerner, B. "Empathy, Need to Change and Improvement with Psychotherapy." *Journal of Consulting Psychology*, 1963. Vol. 27, No. 2, pp. 138-144.

Castaneda, C. *Journey to Ixtlan.* London: Penguin, 1974.

Castaneda, C. *A Separate Reality.* London: Penguin, 1973.

Castaneda, C. *The Teaching of Don Juan: A Yaqui Way of Knowledge.* London: Penguin, 1970.

183

Corey, G., Corey, M., & Callahan, P. 3rd ed., *Issues and Ethics in the Helping Professions*. Pacific Grove, CA: Brooks/Cover, 1988.

Corsini, R., ed. 3rd ed., *Current Psychotherapies*. Illinois: R.E. Peacock Publishers, 1984.

Claxton, G., ed. *Beyond Therapy: The Impact of Eastern Religions on Psychological Theory and Practice.* London: Wisdom Publications, 1986.

Deshimaru, T. *The Zen Way to the Martial Arts: A Japanese Master Reveals the Secrets of the Samurai.* London: Century, 1982.

Dobson, T. "A Kind Word Turneth Away Wrath." *Lomi School Bulletin*, Summer, 1980, pp. 23-24.

Eliade, M. *Shamanism: Archaic Techniques of Ecstasy.* London: Routledge & Kegan Paul, 1982.

Feng, Gia-Fu, & English, J., trans. *Tao Te Ching: A New Translation.* New York: Vintage, 1972.

Frank, J. *Persuasion and Healing: A Comparative Study of Psychotherapy.* Baltimore: The John Hopkins University Press, 1973.

Freud, S. *The Interpretation of Dreams.* In the Collected Works. London: Hogarth Press, 1964.

Freud, S., "Introductory Lectures on Psychoanalysis." Standard Edition, 1963. Vols. 15 and 16.

Goldstein, J. *The Experience of Insight: A Simple and Direct Guide to Buddhist Meditation.* Boulder: Shambhala, 1976.

Goodbread, J. *The Dreambody Toolkit.* New York: Viking-Penguin, 1987.

Hillman, J. and Ventura, M. *We've had a Hundred Years of Psychotherapy and the World's Getting Worse.* San Francisco: HarperCollins, 1992.

Huang, A. *Embrace Tiger, Return to Mountain: The Essence of Tai Chi.* Moab, UT: Real People Press, 1973.

Ingram, D. "Horney's Psychoanalytic Technique," in Kutash and Wolf, eds., 1986, pp. 144-158.

Jung, C.G. "Principles of Practical Psychotherapy." In the *Collected Works*, Vol. 16, London: Routledge & Kegan Paul, 1954.

Jung, C.G. "The Soul and Death." *Structure and Dynamics of the Psyche*, Vol. 8, Princeton: Bollingen Series, 1969.

Jung, C.G. "Psychology and Alchemy." In *Collected Works*, Vol. 12, London: Routledge & Kegan Paul, 1953.

Jung, C.G. "The Aims of Psychotherapy." In *Collected Works*, Vol. 16. London: Routledge & Kegan Paul, 1954.

Jung, C.G. "Psychotherapy and Philosophy of Life." In *Collected Works*, Vol. 16. London: Routledge & Kegan Paul, 1954.

Kaufmann, Y. "Analytical Psychotherapy." In Corsini, ed., *Current Psychotherapies*, 3rd ed. Illinois: F.E. Peacock, 1984.

Kushner, K. *One Arrow, One Life: Zen Archery and Daily Life*. London: Arkana, 1988.

Kutash, I., & Wolf, A., eds. *Psychotherapist's Casebook: Theory and Technique in the Practice of Modern Therapies*. San Francisco: Jossey-Bass, 1986.

Kutash, I., & Greenberg, J. "Psychoanalytic Psychotherapy." In Kutash and Wolf, eds. 1986. pp. 22-42.

London, P. *Modes and Morals of Psychotherapy*. New York: Holt, Reinhard & Winston, 1967.

Masson, J. *Against Therapy: Emotional Tyranny and the Myth of Psychological Healing*. New York: Atheneum, 1988.

Meador, B. & Rogers, C. "Person Centered Therapy." In Corsini, ed. *Current Psychotherapies*, 3rd ed. Tasca, IL: F.E. Peacock, 1984.

Merton, T. *The Way of Chuang Tzu*. New York: New Directions, 1965.

Mikami, T. *Sumi Painting: Study of Japanese Brush Painting*. Tokyo: Shufunotomo, 1965.

Mindell, Amy, & Mindell, Arnold. *Riding the Horse Backwards: Process Oriented Theory and Practice.* London: Penguin(Arkana), 1992.

Mindell, Arnold. *Dreambody: The Body's Role in Revealing the Self.* Boston: Sigo Press, 1982. London & New York: Viking-Penguin, 1986.

Mindell, Arnold. *River's Way: The Process Science of the Dreambody.* London & New York: Viking-Penguin, 1985.

Mindell, Arnold. *Working with the Dreaming Body.* New York & London: Viking-Penguin, 1986.

Mindell, Arnold. *The Dreambody in Relationships.* London and New York: Viking-Penguin, 1987.

Mindell, Arnold. City Shadows: *Psychological Interventions in Psychiatry.* London & New York: Viking-Penguin, 1988.

Mindell, Arnold. *Working on Yourself Alone: Inner Dreambody Work.* London & New York: Viking-Penguin, 1989.

Mindell, Arnold. *The Year One: Global Process Work with Planetary Myths and Structures.* New York & London: Viking-Penguin, 1989.

Mindell, Arnold. *Leader as Martial Artist: An Introduction to Deep Democracy.* San Francisco: HarperCollins, 1992.

Mindell, Arnold. *The Shaman's Body.* San Francisco: Harper Collins, 1993.

Mindell, Arnold. *Coma: The Dreambody Near Death.* London & New York: Viking-Penguin, 1994.

Mindell, Arnold. *Sitting in the Fire: The Politics of Awareness.* To be published, 1995.

Payne, P. *Martial Arts: The Spiritual Dimension.* London: Thames & Hudson, 1981.

Perls, F., Hefferline, R.F. & Goodman, P. *Gestalt Therapy.* New York: Bantam, 1977.

Rawson, P., & Legezo, L. *Tao: The Chinese Philosophy of Time and Change.* London: Thames & Hudson, 1973.

Reid, H., & Crouchet, M. *The Fighting Arts.* New York: Simon & Schuster, 1983.

Rowley, G. *Principles of Chinese Painting.* revised ed. Princeton University Press, 1974.

Strachan, A. "The Wisdom of the Dreaming Body: A Case Study of a Physical Symptom." *Journal of Process Oriented Psychology*, Vol. 5, No. 2, Fall/Winter, Lao Tse Press, 1993.

Strupp, H. & Hadley, S. "Specific vs. Nonspecific. Factors in Psychotherapy: A Controlled Study of Outcome." *Arch. Gen. Psychiatry*, Vol. 36, Sept. 1979, pp. 1125-1136.

Suzuki, D. T. *The Awakening of Zen.* Boston: Shambhala, 1987.

Suzuki, D. T. *Zen and Japanese Culture.* NJ: Princeton University Press, 1973.

Suzuki, S. *Zen Mind, Beginner's Mind: Informal Talks on Zen Meditation and Practice.* New York: Weatherhill, 1970.

Thien-an T. *Zen Philosophy, Zen Practice.* Berkeley: Dharma Publishing & College of Oriental Studies, 1975.

Ueshiba, K. *The Spirit of Aikido.* New York & Tokyo: Kodansha International, 1987.

Walsh, R. & Vaughan, F. *Beyond Ego: Transpersonal Dimensions in Psychology.* Los Angeles: Tarcher, 1980.

Watts, A. *Psychotherapy East and West.* New York: Vintage Books, 1975.

Watts, A. *The Way of Zen.* New York: Vintage Books, 1957.

Wilhelm, R., ed. *I Ching or Book of Changes.* London: Routledge & Kegan Paul, 1973.

Wilson, G. "Behavior Therapy." In Corsini, ed., *Current Psychotherapies*, 3rd ed. Tasca, IL: F.E. Peacock, 1984.

ABOUT THE AUTHOR

Amy Mindell is a dancer, artist, wilderness skier and therapist. Although originally from the United States, she lived in Zurich, Switzerland for ten years, where she met her husband, Arnold Mindell, and studied and practiced process oriented psychology. She has a B.A. in dance and theater, an M.A. in psychology and a Ph.D. in clinical psychology. She is currently in private practice in Portland, Oregon and teaches at the Process Work Center of Portland. She has taught process work in many parts of the world including India, Africa, Japan, Russia, Greece, Poland, England and Australia.

She has been interviewed on *New Dimensions Radio* and *Seeing Beyond Radio*. She is a workshop leader with her husband Arny at such centers as the Omega Institute, Esalen Institute, Frankfurter Ring, Findhorn Institute, and has spoken at and given workshops for conferences held by the Association for Transpersonal Psychology, the Association for Humanistic Psychology, and Common Boundary. She has been an adjunct faculty member of the Institute for Transpersonal Psychology and Antioch International.

She is the co-author of *Riding the Horse Backwards* with Arnold Mindell.

For More Information About Process Oriented Psychology, Contact:

The Process Work Center of Portland
733 NW Everett, Box 11, Suite 3C
Portland, OR 97209
U.S.A.
telephone: (503) 223-8188
fax: (503) 227-7003

Journal of Process Oriented Psychology
Lao Tse Press
P.O. Box 40206
Portland, OR 97240-0206
U.S.A.
telephone: (503) 222-3778
fax: (503) 222-3782

Research Society for Process Oriented Psychology
Binzstr. 9
8045 Zurich,
Switzerland
telephone: 41-1-451-2070
fax: 41-1-451-2090

Other Titles From New Falcon Publications

Secrets of Western Tantra
The Tree of Lies
Undoing Yourself With Energized Meditation
    By Christopher S. Hyatt, Ph.D.
The Enochian World of Aleister Crowley
    By Aleister Crowley, L. M. DuQuette, and C. S. Hyatt
Pacts With The Devil
    By S. J. Black and Christopher. S. Hyatt, Ph.D.
Urban Voodoo
    By Christopher. S. Hyatt, Ph.D. and S. J. Black
Eight Lectures on Yoga
Gems From the Equinox
Pathworkings of Aleister Crowley: The Treasure House of Images
    By Aleister Crowley
Secrets of the Shaman
    By Gini Graham Scott, Ph.D.
Monsters & Magical Sticks: There's No Such Thing as Hypnosis?
    By Steven Heller, Ph.D.
Neuropolitique
Info-Psychology
The Game of Life
    By Timothy Leary, Ph.D.
Zen Without Zen Masters
    By Camden Benares
The Complete Golden Dawn System of Magic
The Eye in the Triangle
Golden Dawn Tapes: Series I, II, and III
    By Israel Regardie
Carl Sagan and Immanuel Velikovsky
    By Charles Ginenthal
Soul Magic: Understanding Your Journey
    By Katherine Torres, Ph.D.
Astrology and Consciousness: The Wheel of Light
    By Rio Olesky
Between Duality: The Art of Transcendence
    By Laurence Galian

And to get your free catalog of *all* of our titles, write to:

NEW FALCON PUBLICATIONS (Catalog Dept.)
1739 East Broadway Road Suite 1-277
Tempe, AZ 85282 U.S.A.